P9-AQH-281

Collected Poems of Yvor Winters

ALSO BY YVOR WINTERS

CRITICISM

In Defense of Reason
Edwin Arlington Robinson
The Function of Criticism
Forms of Discovery
The Uncollected Essays and Reviews
(ed. Francis Murphy)

POETRY

Collected Poems
The Early Poems

EDITOR

Twelve Poets of the Pacific
Poets of the Pacific, *Second Series*
The Quest for Reality
(with Kenneth Fields)

The Collected Poems of

YVOR WINTERS

with an introduction by Donald Davie

Carcanet · Manchester

Published by
The Swallow Press, Inc.
811 W. Junior Terrace
Chicago, Illinois 60613

ISBN 0-8040-0799-3
Library of Congress catalog card Number 78-51596
LIBRARY OF CONGRESS CATALOG CARD NUMBER 78-51596

The Publishers would like to thank Janet Lewis, the wife of Yvor Winters, for her help and guidance in preparing this book.

CONTENTS

*Those early poems marked by an asterisk were later included by Winters in the 1960 edition of his *Collected Poems*, and will be found in Part Two of this volume. The relevant page number is given in brackets. *See* Note on Text, p. 8.

*The poems which follow 'Marine' and precede 'The Slow Pacific Swell' are from *The Proof*, 1930. The next poems preceding 'Anacreontic' are from *The Journey*, 1931. From 'Anacreontic' to 'Chiron' inclusive, and one poem excepted, the poems come from *Before Disaster*, 1934. Other poems first appeared in *Poems*, 1940, *The Giant Weapon*, 1943, and *Three Poems*, 1950.

THE POETRY OF YVOR WINTERS

THE FUNDAMENTAL distinction among English-language poets—the one of the coarsest mesh, but the one that the working poet daily lives with and operates by—is not any distinction between Romantic and Classicist, between rationalist and irrationalist, between a strict kind of formalist and the loose or 'organic' kind. The fundamental, the radical split is between those who think that a poem is a considered utterance, and those who think it is unconsidered.

Nobody, one might think, has ever seriously advanced a theory of poetry as unconsidered utterance. But on the contrary such a position has been, and is, defended repeatedly. And the defences available range from some that are self-evidently fatuous to others that are sophisticated and superficially plausible. Among the more sophisticated, for instance, are those theories that start from the proposition that over by far the greater range of his daily activities modern man is required to be all too 'considering', that at every point man and woman in our technologically advanced societies are required to calculate, to anticipate consequences, to reckon up the odds. This necessity (so the argument develops) thwarts and chokes our capacities for spontaneous behaviour, so that for instance even our sexual behaviour becomes calculated, all too monstrously 'considered'. On this showing poetry has a duty to be 'unconsidered', at least in some respects and to some notable degree, because only by being so can it discharge its therapeutic and social duty to defend such threatened areas of experience as our sexuality.

Yvor Winters was always sure—whether he was writing his unparaphrasable lyrics in the 1920s, or the later partly paraphrasable poems by which he is better known—that a poem is a considered utterance, indeed that some great poems may well be the most considered utterances that mankind has yet shown itself capable of. But we mustn't suppose that Winters didn't know the arguments on the other side, or that he thought they had no weight. He might have pointed out that language, the medium poets work in, is far from being a product of consideration; that on the contrary it is the product of quite exuberant spontaneity, continuous and continuing.

This is more conspicuously true of English, the language of Shakespeare, than of the Romance languages. (And Winters, it is not often realized, when he began his study of Renaissance poetry, began with poems in Spanish, not English.) Thus the poet who seeks to make of his poems considered utterances is in fruitful tension with his medium, because that medium, his language, will always be budding out in multivalences, double meanings and ambiguities under his very hands. It might even be true to say that in this conflict the language of Shakespeare always in the end defeats the poet; the finished poem, because it is the product of the language as much as of the poet, will *never* be as clear, as exact and conclusive, as the poet dreamed it might be. And if so, the attempt to make considered utterances can never do damage, precisely because in the last analysis the attempt must always to some degree fail. Which doesn't mean however that the attempt, since it is foredoomed, was by that token misconceived. On the contrary, from poems that attempt only to *go along* with language, happily accepting the patterns that language throws up of its own accord (for instance the intriguing verbal doodles and sometimes intricate jingles that come into one's head between sleeping and waking), there will always be missing precisely the tension that comes of the artificer bending his will against his medium, going against the grain of it. And nothing can make up for that lack. Moreover, what is true of the semantics of English is true also of its other dimension as patterned sound and sequences of sound; and here the argument makes for meter against free verse.

These reflections are all mine, my impressions from remembering Winters the man as I knew him, and from pondering the poems which he wrote. I am not paraphrasing any page of his criticism, for as critic Winters approached these questions in a very different way—though that way led him, I believe, to very similar conclusions. In any case it is advisable—I might even say, it is absolutely necessary—to suppress whatever one may know of Winters's criticism, when approaching his poems. That is the only way for those poems to get a fair hearing. And because on both sides of the Atlantic nearly every one of the few who have read Winters's poetry, have done so only after first reading in his criticism, it is almost true to say that Winters's poems have never yet had a fair hearing. It is not the case of course that Winters's criticism points one way, his poetry another. The poems and the criticism can be matched up, right enough; and the one can be made to validate the other. But what an eccentric and impoverished and mean-spirited way that is, of reading poetry! Winters's poems are considered utterances, to be sure; but what they have considered, and now utter, is not such or such a contested and challenging position in poetic theory or literary history, but the matter of what it is like to be human, the pains and the pleasures of it—of being a man acting in history, acting in society (a highly specific and sharply specified society), acting in landscapes (some landscapes rather than others, and those exactly described), and acting in a web of human relationships and the responsibilities which those impose. Winters's poems were not written for class-room use or for polemical purposes; they were composed and made public not as models or *exempla* or illustrations of 'how to write', but as considered statements of how to *live*, or of how the business of living had been experienced by one thoughtful and feelingful man. That awkward amphibian the poet-critic runs the danger, which Winters certainly has not escaped, of having the poet in him immolated for the sake of the critic. And whether the immolation is for the purpose of exalting the critic or decrying him, hardly matters; in either case the poet has been denied the sort of attention which we readily give to poets who either aren't critics at all, or else self-evidently foolish and careless ones. We may go further, and ask: what is the poet inside the poet-critic doing, if not outwitting the critic in him? There are things happening in Winters's poetry that were not dreamed of in his criticism; if it were not so, why should he have bothered writing the poems at all?

Winters had a proper contempt for the parochialism which, lacking historical perspective and historical knowledge, regards the particular span of years that we are living through as unprecedented—for no better reason than because we, such specially interesting people as we are, happen to be living in it. For that sort of know-nothing 'modernism' he had nothing but impatient scorn. But that does not mean that, as he wrote his poems, he thought of himself as anything but the creature of a particular geographical place at a particular historical time. His 'View of Pasadena from the Hills' is every inch a twentieth-century Californian poem, as its title indicates. But it is not therefore *provincial*; for the depletion which the poem mourns, of one particular Californian landscape, is only an instance of a depletion—rather, a rape—that other landscapes have suffered in the present century. I remember him making the point quietly but firmly, with reference to this particular poem of his, when in the last months of his life he and I were reading Hardy's poems together, and I had reflected mournfully on what had transformed the landscapes of Hardy's Wessex since Hardy died. Because Winters never travelled outside the United States, and through the latter part of his life could only with difficulty be prevailed upon to leave the environs of San Francisco, it is assumed that his knowledge of other parts of the earth's surface—particularly of the mediterranean Europe from which (so he maintained, very unfashionably) American culture derived—could only have been, in a damaging and emasculating sense, 'literary'. Thus, when he writes in his 'Anacreontic',

> Peace! there is peace at last.
> Deep in the Tuscan shade,
> Swathed in the Grecian past,
> Old Landor's bones are laid . . .

it is easy to come up with the glib and canting objection: Since he'd never been to either Tuscany or Greece, how could the words, 'Tuscan' and 'Grecian', have for him anything but a merely *verbal* significance? Even as I say that it is easy to raise the objection, I cudgel my memory in vain for any one who has raised it. Which is a pity; because the objection forces us to find an answer which is surprising and touching, and therefore illuminating. By way of answer I read from 'In Praise of California Wines':

> With pale bright leaf and shadowy stem,
> Pellucid amid nervous dust,
> By pre-Socratic stratagem,
> Yet sagging with its weight of must,
>
> The vineyard spreads beside the road
> In repetition, point and line.

I sing, in this dry bright abode,
The praises of the native wine.

It yields the pleasure of the eye,
It charms the skin, it warms the heart;
When nights are cold and thoughts crowd high,
Then 'tis the solvent for our art.

When worn for sleep the head is dull,
When art has failed us, far behind,
Its sweet corruption fills the skull
Till we are happy to be blind.

So may I yet, as poets use,
My time being spent, and more to pay,
In this quick warmth the will diffuse,
In sunlight vanish quite away.

'As poets use' . . . the very usage of 'use' is archaic. But what has the poem been saying, if not that it has a right to such archaisms, as also to ''tis' and numerous inversions of the order of spoken American? Every one knows that California has a mediterranean climate; not everyone knows that the climate has produced, insofar as California has produced any indigenous culture or 'life-style' at all, a mediterranean style of life—in which for instance the culture of the grape plays a central role. Winters has a right to the words 'Tuscan' and 'Grecian', and to the time-honoured locutions which those words summon up as their appropriate accompaniments, because the landscape and the climate which Landor encountered as soon as he stepped outside his door in Florence are identical with the climate and landscape that Winters walked into as soon as he stepped towards his little orchard in Los Altos. What I am saying is that one of the strongest impulsions behind Winters's poetry is the Virgilian *pietas*—towards a native or adopted (in Winters's case, adopted) terrain. And if we ask what place there is, in Winters's critical theory, for such an irrationally powerful sentiment and impulsion, the answer has to be, so far as I can see: no place at all—which is just one example of how the poetry traffics in realities that the criticism knows nothing of. As myself an adopted Californian I put it on record that the California I move about in is more redolently and vividly present in Winters's poems—and in their way of saying, as much as in what they say—than in any of the much-touted urban poets of San Francisco and Los Angeles, or in the self-consciously rural and 'opting out' poems of Gary Snyder.

Before this archaic yet so lately fabricated backdrop, there are enacted dramas which are similarly archaic and yet urgently topical—the drama, for instance, of David Lamson, accused of murdering his wife. Or there is 'Before Disaster', dated *Winter, 1932-3*;

Evening traffic homeward burns,
Swift and even on the turns,
Drifting weight in triple rows,
Fixed relation and repose.
This one edges out and by,
Inch by inch with steady eye.
But should error be increased,
Mass and moment are released;
Matter loosens, flooding blind,
Levels drivers to its kind.
  Ranks of nations thus descend,
Watchful to a stormy end.
By a moment's calm beguiled,
I have got a wife and child.
Fool and scoundrel guide the State.
Peace is whore to Greed and Hate.
Nowhere may I turn to flee:
Action is security.
Treading change with savage heel,
We must live or die by steel.

Wherever I have read this poem in the English-speaking world, I have heard objections raised to what is called the 'stilted rhetoric' of the second half—particularly, so some of my listeners have said, when it comes on the heel of Winters's early but conclusive treatment of what it feels like to drive on a multi-lane freeway. Such objections, it seems to me, come not out of any perception of the poem as a rhetorically consistent because considered statement, but out of a pre-judgment about the English-speaking societies of our time or of the 1930s. The poet assumes that those societies are worthy to be judged, and of course castigated, in a vocabulary and by standards not wholly out of touch with those by and in which Juvenal judged Domitian's Rome, and Dryden judged William III's London. He pays his society that compliment. But such a compliment is harder to forgive than any insult. Because we are (we suppose) unprecedented, or in unprecedented situations, we demand to be judged by standards peculiar to—which is to say, more lenient than—the standards by which societies of the past were judged and castigated by *their* poets. I will not pretend that all Winters's archaisms of diction and rhetoric can be justified in this way; but certainly sometimes we jib at them because we are not prepared to be called for judgment at the bar of the centuries and the millennia.

Winters, I would say, is not a good model for young poets of today to emulate. He cannot be such a model precisely because he is so much a poet of his nation, his region, and his time—a conjunction which, in the nature of things, can never recur. Yet this does not mean that he is 'dated'. On the contrary his achievement is, through his style, to have enforced the generally acknowledged but in particular cases always unacceptable paradox that the more rootedly particular poems are—think of Thomas Hardy!—the more universal their significance.

DONALD DAVIE

NOTE ON THE TEXT

Parts One and Two of the present volume are based on *The Early Poems of Yvor Winters 1920-28* (Alan Swallow, 1966) and *Collected Poems* (Alan Swallow, 1960) respectively. To avoid repetition, the early poems which were retained by Winters in the *Collected Poems* have, with a few exceptions, been omitted from Part One. In the Contents the titles of the omitted poems have been asterisked and are given in their original position so that the sequence followed in *The Early Poems of Yvor Winters 1920-28* should be clear. The *Collected Poems* are given intact in Part Two in order that Winters's 'definition by example' should be preserved.

Part Three consists of poems and translations which have appeared in print but not been collected. It contains some translations from *Poems* (Gyroscope Press, 1940), other translations which Winters wished to be kept, and a group of twelve poems which are given in chronological order. The text of the privately printed pamphlet *Diadems and Fagots* (1920) is given entire, and includes some translations by John Meem of the Brazilian poet Olavo Bilac.

Part Four consists of the short story 'The Brink of Darkness'.

I/EARLY POEMS

INTRODUCTION

I PUBLISH this book* to provide an authorized edition of my early and 'experimental' work. Some one would do this in any event, and probably some one who would sweep all of my uncollected work into a single volume, with no indication of what I had considered my best work as I was writing and publishing it. I include three small books, a group of four poems previously uncollected from magazines, and two later groups of some size. The first of these later groups, the 'Fire Sequence', appeared in *The American Caravan* of 1927; the second formed the first section of my volume *The Proof* (1930). The 'Fire Sequence' contained two poems written later and about another landscape, and these will be found in the final group where they belong; they are 'Incandescent Earth' and 'Orange Tree'. The final group originally contained a few other poems reprinted from the 'Fire Sequence', and these I have left in the 'Fire Sequence' and have omitted from the final group, which is miscellaneous. Except for these few details of arrangement and the inclusion of a group of four poems previously uncollected, I have done no editing and I have revised no poems. Any other uncollected material is rubbish. I wish to be clear on two points: I regard this work as inferior to my later work; I regard it as very good of its kind, quite as good as any of the 'experimental' work of this century. In any collection as large as this and written within so few years, there will be some bad poems; I think that I can identify these, but I do not believe that the incidence is high. In order to present the record, I have retained them.

These poems can best be clarified by a little autobiographical detail; I will try to keep it to a minimum.

I became interested in poetry and the writing of poetry at the age of fourteen. In my last year of high school, at the age of sixteen, I discovered Miss Monroe's magazine, then called by its original name: *Poetry: A Magazine of Verse*, and I became a subscriber. In McClurg's Book Store in Chicago I discovered copies of *The Little Review* and of *Others*, and began purchasing them, and it was at this time (and place) that I

*This introduction was written for *The Early Poems of Yvor Winters 1920-28* (Alan Swallow, 1966).

bought a fair number of books by Yeats, Pound, Williams, and other moderns. I became acquainted with the work of Stevens in high school, long before the publication of *Harmonium* in 1923. I entered the University of Chicago in the fall of 1917, and became a member of the recently formed Poetry Club. This was a very intelligent group, worth more than most courses in literature; among the new members were Glenway Wescott, a year younger than myself, who, like myself, had discovered most of the unknown moderns in high school, and Elizabeth Madox Roberts, about twenty years our elder. Janet Lewis, later to become my wife, joined the group the following year, but after I had left the university. Through this group I made the acquaintance of Miss Monroe, who encouraged me to visit her in her office. She was usually busy when I called, and I read old issues of *Poetry* and books in her large collection of modern verse and criticism; occasionally other visitors came by, some of them interesting. Shortly before I left the university in the following winter, Miss Monroe, who had been sorting out her files in the hope of finding more space on her shelves, gave me a complete set of duplicates of the first six or seven volumes of the magazine, enough to bring me up to the point at which my subscription began. At the end of the autumn quarter of 1918, I discovered that I had tuberculosis and was taken to California, the home of my childhood, for a few weeks, and then to Santa Fé, New Mexico, where I remained until late October of 1921, most of the time in bed in a sanatorium. I took my files of *Poetry* and my books of modern poetry with me, and I subscribed to *Others* and *The Little Review*, and, as occasion permitted, to a few later and similar magazines. These magazines and a few books were my chief sources of education during a period of five years. Alice Corbin Henderson, Miss Monroe's assistant, had preceded me to Santa Fé with the same disease; I shortly made her acquaintance, and she lent me books and advised me. Late in 1921 or a little after, I made the acquaintance of Marianne Moore by mail; she was then a librarian in the New York Public Library, and she sent me books, very kindly but I am sure illegally. The books sent me by Miss Moore were all books that I needed to read, but they were chosen with a typical disregard of historical or other classification; I remember reading *The Golden Bowl*, at the age of twenty-one and with no preparation, while I was a teacher in a coal-mining camp. And there was a French priest in Santa Fé who gave me a few, and my first, lessons in French, lessons which set me to work at a frustrating effort to decipher Rimbaud, a poet of whom my friend the priest thoroughly disapproved.

The Immobile Wind and nearly all of *The Magpie's Shadow* were written while I was at the sanatorium in Santa Fé. I believe that two poems in *The Bare Hills*, 'The Impalpable Void' and 'The Fragile Season', were written toward the end of the same period. There was no French influence on these poems, except as it might have filtered through the Imagists or perhaps through Stevens or Sturge Moore. I had been reading Bridges and Hardy, whom I admired but who did not influence me at this time, and Emily Dickinson and Adelaide Crapsey, who may have influenced me. I was familiar also with many translations from the poetry of the Japanese and of the American Indians; the Indians especially were an influence on *The Magpie's Shadow*.

In October of 1921, I left the sanatorium and went to Ranchos de Taos, where I stayed with friends for a few weeks. I then went to Madrid, a coal-mining camp about twenty miles south of Santa Fé, where I taught in the grade school for a year. The name of the town was not pronounced as we would pronounce it; it was *Mad*-rid. That is, in English; the Mexicans, when speaking their native language, gave it the correct Spanish pronunciation. Madrid was in a long, narrow, and deep valley, a shark's-mouth, about three miles into the mountains from Los Cerrillos, the railroad outlet for the mines. Los Cerrillos had been a Mexican village before the mines came; the houses in Madrid were frame shacks, all of them painted a light harsh blue, the houses of Cerrillos were adobe. The coal was mined in Madrid; the brothels and dispensaries of illegal liquor (this was in the days of Prohibition) were in Cerrillos. The high school also was in Cerrillos, and I taught there the following year; there were six boys in the high school and I think two girls. Accidents, many fatal, were common in the mines, from which union organizers were vigorously excluded and sometimes removed; drunken violence was a daily and nightly occurrence in both towns; mayhem and murder were discussed with amusement. Yet I was treated with deference: I was able to keep order at the public dances on Friday nights merely by my presence until ten o'clock, but after ten, because of the consumption of liquor, I needed (and received) the assistance of the marshal. The miners tipped their hats to me when they passed me in the street; the Mexicans addressed me as Maestro, the others as Professor.

In the spring of 1923 I left for the University of Colorado at Boulder, where I enrolled as a second-quarter sophomore for the summer quarter. After nine consecutive quarters, including three summer quarters, I received a B.A. and an M.A. in Romance Languages, with a minor in Latin. My training in the languages, and especially in philology, was excellent; my training in literature was nil. Before the end of the first year I was reading extensively in French literature and was making a beginning on the Symbolists, who were not in the curriculum; by the end of my second year I read French and Spanish very easily, including Old French and Old Spanish; I was a fair Latinist and had read a good deal of Vergil, Ovid, Horace, and Catullus and less of a few other poets, and knew some Italian, but I could not speak French or Spanish well enough to teach them. Nevertheless, in my ignorance, I went to the University of Idaho at Moscow, in the northern end of the state, where I taught French and Spanish for two years. Boulder was a big enough city to have a street-car line, and it was an hour or so from Denver; Moscow was too small for a street-car line and the only cities were at least half a day away and were small besides. The library at Moscow was almost nothing, but it contained a couple of standard sets of Iberian literature which enabled me to read extensively in Old Spanish, Old Portuguese (Galician, gallego), and in the Spanish poetry of the Renaissance. I read all of Proust, most of Flaubert, and other French prose, and continued my reading of the Symbolists. By the end of 1927 I knew French literature fairly well and had a passable knowledge of Spanish. My knowledge of English and American literature before the modern period was very slight.

In the summer of 1926 I was married to Janet Lewis in

Santa Fé. She also had gone there because of her health, and she was not well enough to return to Moscow with me, so I went alone. The following summer we both went to California, and I entered Stanford University as a graduate student in English in the autumn of 1927.

The first poems in this collection were written early in 1920, when I was nineteen years of age; the last were written early in 1928, when I was twenty-seven; they are the work of eight years or a little less, and are the work of a young man. They deal with my experience in the places which I have named, and were written with the knowledge which I have indicated. The 'Fire Sequence' was written during my last winter at Moscow, but dealt with Madrid in retrospect. In the 'twenties I was not in Paris, nor even at Harvard. After a year as a student at Stanford, I became a full-time instructor of English, but continued my studies and completed my doctorate; I have remained on the same English faculty since, but retire in June of 1966. I had no opportunity to study English literature before coming to Stanford, nor the history of criticism, nor the 'history of ideas' generally.

Early in 1928 I abandoned free verse and returned to traditional meters. This was not due to the influence of Stanford nor to any sudden intellectual or religious conversion. It was becoming increasingly obvious to me that the poets whom I most admired were Baudelaire and Valéry, and Hardy, Bridges, and Stevens in a few poems each, and that I could never hope to approach the quality of their work by the method which I was using. I changed my method, explored the new method, and gradually came to understand the theoretical reasons for the change which I had made as a practical necessity. I perhaps should point out also that my theory of the scansion of free verse was worked out toward the end of my last year at Moscow, when most of my free verse had been written. There are a good many critics today who believe that all of my poetry has been governed by principles worked out in advance and then put mechanically into practice. Actually, I wrote as anyone writes, with what intelligence I could muster at the time, improving my intelligence as I went along. During my first year at Stanford, I took the usual courses in Old and Middle English; I discovered that for me English poetry began with Chaucer, although I was grateful for such knowledge as I acquired of earlier poetry and even for the poor training which I received in English philology. I read Chaucer and the Scots Chaucerians systematically and began a systematic reading of English poetry from Skelton onward to Bridges and Hardy, and of American as well. I missed few poets of importance, I am sure, during the eight or nine years in which this was my principal occupation, and I have reread many a good many times. This reading disclosed two more poets, Fulke Greville and Ben Jonson, who have remained with the five already mentioned, among the poets who move me most profoundly, and the passage of time has produced two more, both too much younger than myself to have influenced me, but very great poets, J. V. Cunningham and Edgar Bowers. And there have been isolated poems by other men: 'Church Monuments', for example, by George Herbert, and 'The Cricket', by F. G. Tuckerman.

One final word of warning. My shift from the methods of these early poems to the methods of my later was not a shift from formlessness to form; it was a shift from certain kinds of form to others. I was aware of form (when it occurred) in the work of other writers from an early date and was always preoccupied to achieve it in my own work. Form is something that one perceives or does not perceive; theory in itself is insufficient. But theory is helpful as a guide, and some persons can acquire a measure of perception with the help of theory, and this fact provides an excuse for the existence of critics and teachers. When I say that these poems had form, I refer not only to the possibility that the free verse may be scanned by my method, perhaps with difficulty; I refer to the fact that these poems are rhythmical, not merely from line to line, but in total movement from beginning to end, and that the relations between the meanings of the parts is an element in the rhythm, along with the sound. In the long run, however, the free verse and the associational procedure in the use of imagery and in the interrelation of images and other passages proved severely restrictive. In the last two groups, especially, in this collection, the movement, and consequently the diction, were often violent; form dictated the state of mind and often the subject, and these were not always intelligent. Sometimes the subject justified the state of mind and the form, but not always, and some poems are exceptions to what I have just said. Some of the best poems in the collection and some of the worst are in these two groups. But I had pushed this method past the limits of its efficaciousness, and for reasons which I have discussed in my criticism I found myself unable to write what I wished, and I therefore changed my method.*

From first to last, most of my favorite poets have been relatively modern, and my matter and my methods have been modern. At no time in my later work did I try to emulate the Elizabethans or the poets of the eighteenth century or to revive their methods, despite the theories of various critics. My aim from the first poem in this collection was a clean and accurate diction and movement, free of clichés; in other respects my methods have altered with the years.

Y. W.

*One poem in the last group does not belong there chronologically; 'The Goatherds' was written in the summer of 1923, just after I had arrived in Boulder from Cerrillos. The scene of the poem is near Cerrillos. For some reason I did not include the poem in *The Bare Hills*, but published it later in *The Proof*.

THE IMMOBILE WIND (1921)

TWO SONGS OF ADVENT

I.
On the desert, between pale mountains, our cries—
Far whispers creeping through an ancient shell.

II.
Coyote, on delicate mocking feet,
Hovers down the canyon, among the mountains,
His voice running wild in the wind's valleys.

Listen! listen! for I enter now your thought.

ONE RAN BEFORE

I could tell
Of silence where
One ran before
Himself and fell
Into silence
Yet more fair.

And this were more
A thing unseen
Than falling screen
Could make of air.

HAWK'S EYES

As a gray hawk's eyes
Turn here and away,
So my course turns
Where I walk each day.

BALLAD

I sat alone.
Lest thought might fail
Down the fine road of day.

I sat alone.
The swinging flail
Of men will never stay.

I sat alone.
A blade of grass was pale,
Like a woman far away.

THE IMMOBILE WIND

Blue waves within the stone
Turn like deft wrists interweaving.

Emotion, undulant, alone.
Curled wings flow beyond perceiving.

Swift points of sight,
mystic and amorous little hands,
The wind has drunk
as water swallows sifting sands.

The wings of a butterfly
Feel of the wind
Tentatively, as men die
In thought, that have not sinned.

THE PRIESTHOOD

We stand apart
That men may see
The lines about our eyes.

We perish, we
Who die in art,
With that surprise

Of one who speaks
To us and knows
Wherein he lies.

THE MORNING

The dragonfly
Is deaf and blind
That burns across
The morning.

And silence dinned
Is but a scream
Of fear until
One turns in dream.

I see my kind
That try to turn:
I see one thin
Man running.

WHERE MY SIGHT GOES

Who knows
Where my sight goes,
What your sight shows—
Where the peachtree blows?

The frogs sing
Of everything,
And children run
As leaves swing.

And many women pass
Dressed in white,
As thoughts of noon pass
From sea to sea.

And all these things would take
My life from me.

BALLAD OF MEN

Like long clouds
On the skyline,
All day men come to me.
I stand and watch them sidewise
In thought eternally.

And if men pass
They pass like birds
With necks craning aside.
And when they pass I know that You
Or they or I have lied.

And all my life
And all my sight
Are scattered like green sea.
There is death in women walking.
Thus I come unto Thee.

TWO DRAMATIC INTERLUDES FOR PUPPETS

I. *Autumn Roadside*

Scene: An old road runs the length of the stage, with a thin row of pine trees parallel to it and a little way back. A stream comes from the pines and crosses it at the left. On the far side of the road, beside the stream, sit two puppets. One, with his back turned three-quarters to the audience, is dressed in dull intense blue. The other, facing the audience, is dressed in black, with a black cape attached to his arms, and has a black face with dull blue lips and dull red eyes. At the front and right of the stage is a little tree with a few withered leaves. It is twilight.

Blue Puppet
I sit and whisper, and the sea,
A drifting feather, sinks to me.

Black Puppet
Beneath my bent eyes water flows
Obliquely to my slanting nose.

Blue Puppet, raising his head
Cry to the twilight,
Cry to the twilight,
It flew, a long arrow,
And buried itself in the west.
Its feathers flicker
Like a poplar's crest.

Black Puppet
Night lies, a battered shield,
Against the eastern hill.
The soul of twilight is insects singing,
Still, still.
My hands are like autumn waters running—

Blue Puppet, rising to feet, and, toward end of speech, walking back and forth rapidly
Day is water of green sea
Within a ball of glass.
I saw light run upon the ripples
As I ran upon a ground of brass.

The sun was a tiny golden fly within it,
Frightened; and I cried in fear;
And I ran about in circles
On the brazen ground beneath,
My cold feet falling clear.

Then I fled through time like the arrow of twilight—

Black Puppet, rising
The black beetle walks from the hills of night
To take the evening in his hands;
But the waters spread, and drift into the night,
Green waters, falling from his hands.

A man runs down from the hills beneath the sun
Crying words unknown and clear;
And I cry for pain to enter him and run his course—

He strikes Blue Puppet, who falls dead
And I enter and cry in fear.

I stand with my hands within the waters of the day—
They fall like sunrays in long lines;
My eyes are shadows on the pines.—

He stands silent for a moment, then sinks to ground, speaking
But a bluebird
Turned his wing
Across my eyes,
Hastening.

I did not know
I saw him go
Till I glanced
Down the stream.

For the falling of a bird
The harsh sound of feet on leaves
Mocks a tune that I once heard.

Now I rise and turn my eyes
Toward old autumn places.

He passes beneath the little tree, drawing cloak across his face

The smooth sharpness of a dangling leaf,
Struggling with receding sap within,
Is like a face that hides its grief.

Curtain.

II. *The Pines are Shadows*

Scene: Same as for 'Autumn Roadside'. White Puppet and Black Puppet walk in from the right, the former slightly ahead and on the side near the audience. They walk across the stage, speaking, and pausing occasionally; the last speech is almost off-stage to the left.

White Puppet
My life is green water seen
Through a white rose leaf.
It has a sheen.

Black Puppet
A dry leaf on the ground
Is much like me.
It turns around
And then lies still.

White Puppet
Your eyes are like
Such a leaf.
I wish you ill.

Black Puppet
Yonder stream is shaken
Like a butterfly's antenna.

White Puppet
I have watched its life awaken
As it shivers in the dew.

Black Puppet
A clinging silver shadow
Bends a grass-blade to the ground.
The ants walk through
And they walk around.

White Puppet
My mind is a white bird
Like the sun above—
Death is only
The shadows thereof.
They fall in lines
And they interlace—

Black Puppet
And yet you say a wisdom
Is across my face.

White Puppet
You have seen Coyote
Who flows like gold,
The runner in the night
With eartips like the air.

Black Puppet
Coyote is green eyes
On dust whirl of yellow hair—
My passion is untold.

White Puppet
Coyote is an ether
That is shaken in the air.
He hovers about me
When the day is white.
He passes swifter
Than the runner in the night.

Black Puppet
My passion is untold.

White Puppet
I rose and leaned
With pines against the sky.
And I felt the tiny ripples
As the day flowed by.

Black Puppet
I walked down the road at dusk—
The dust pulled at my feet.

White Puppet
I saw far below me
The falling yellow wheat.

Black Puppet
The wind, a wounded rabbit,
Dragged itself beneath a pinyon;
And I looked into the eyes
Of the chipmunk morning.

White Puppet
Sunlight falls
Across my hair
As leaves fall
On the water.

Exit White Puppet slowly, hands raised.

Black Puppet, sinking to ground
He who knoweth, listeneth;
I turn about and hear again—

My hair is smooth with death
And whirls above my brain.

DEATH GOES BEFORE ME

Death goes before me on his hands and knees,
And we go down among the bending trees.

Weeping I go, and no man gives me ease—
I am that strange thing that each strange eye sees.

Eyes of the silence and all life an eye
Turn in the wind, and always I walk by.

Too still I go, and all things go from me
As down far autumn beaches a man runs to the sea.

My hands are cold, my lips are thin and dumb.
Stillness is like the beating of a drum.

THE WIZARD

I am the wizard of the golden hills.
Do not believe in me, nor in the mills

Turning in fallen leaves and in my hair;
Lest I cry, 'End this thing!' And all my rare

Life—all the falling hill-fields, thou too, thou
Who long to walk on paling fields—say how

It came to be, and turn in my own sight,
Gather and vanish, fleeing Israelite.

MY MEMORY

My memory is falling
Like the snow—
Oh, know thyself in memory
Ere death shall know!

I found thought ever walking
Through a distant door;
I found sheer women talking
Like surf on a shore.

Eyes alone, I watched my feet,
Lifted hands and saw them fall;
Thought of distance, running thin,
Bore me as upon a pall

Out of life and into death
With unknown train:
Though thy brother hearkeneth
Return were vain.

THE CHAPEL

Like hour of death
I entered in,
Before I knew the cost.

The altar's form,
Though seen of men,
I polished until lost.

And I shall not
Turn eyes again
Toward my own face of frost.

I PAVED A SKY

I paved a sky
   With days.
I crept beyond the Lie.
   This phrase,
Yet more profound,
   Grew where
I was not: I
   Was there.

A woman came
   Down thin
Valleys, scarlet-flowered;
   Nor in
Nor out my name.

I never know
Where to stand.
I turn and go,
   Increasing, numb,
Of them who thumb
   Their lives
From land to land.

THE MAGPIE'S SHADOW (1922)

O saisons, ô châteaux!

I. IN WINTER

Myself
Pale mornings, and
I rise.

Still Morning
Snow air—my fingers curl.

Awakening
New snow, O pine of dawn!

Winter Echo
Thin air! My mind is gone.

The Hunter
Run! In the magpie's shadow.

No Being
I, bent. Thin nights receding.

II. IN SPRING

Spring
I walk out the world's door.

May
Oh, evening in my hair!

Spring Rain
My doorframe smells of leaves.

Song
Why should I stop
  for spring?

III. IN SUMMER AND AUTUMN

Sunrise
Pale bees! O whither now?

Fields
I did not pick
  a flower.

At Evening
Like leaves my feet passed by.

Cool Nights
At night bare feet on flowers!

Sleep
Like winds my eyelids close.

The Aspen's Song
The summer holds me here.

The Walker
In dream my feet are still.

Blue Mountain
A deer walks that mountain.

God of Roads
I, peregrine of noon.

September
Faint gold! O think not here.

A Lady
She's sun on autumn leaves.

Alone
I saw day's shadow strike.

A Deer
The trees rose in the dawn.

Man in Desert
His feet run as eyes blink.

Desert
The tented autumn, gone!

The End
Dawn rose, and desert shrunk.

High Valleys
In sleep I filled these lands.

Awaiting Snow
The well of autumn—dry.

THE BARE HILLS (1927)

I. UPPER RIVER COUNTRY: RIO GRANDE

Les oiselès de mon païs
Ai oïs en Bretaigne . . .

I. *Hill Burial*

Goatherds inevitable as stones
And rare
As stones observed.

Jesús Leal
Who aimed at solitude,
The only mean,
Was borne by men.

Wet air,
The air of stone.

He sank to God.

III. *The Resurrection*

Spring penetrated
Slowly
To the doorstep
Where the snow
Lay in gray patches—
March was pale.

The stallion
Stood like water
In cold shade
On riven soil.
The trees were bare as glass
About the open doors.

Leal was dead.
And still his wife
Carried in pinelogs
Split and yellow like a man's hair—
Wet earth, shadow of the winter,
Motionless beside the door.

IV. *Tewa Spring*

Red spring
In deep valleys

The peachtree
Lies in shadow
Deep as stone

The river
Is unheard

V. *Dark Spring*

My mother
Foresaw deaths
And walked among
Chrysanthemums,
Winecolored,
Withered rose,
The earthy blossoms.

My very breath
Disowned
In nights of study,
And page by page
I came on spring.

The rats run on the roof,
These words come hard—
Sadder than cockcrow
In a dreamless, earthen sleep.
The Christ, eternal
In the scented cold; my love,
Her hand on the sill
White, as if out of earth;
And spring, the sleep of the dead.

VI. *The Crystal Sun*

Lean spring came in,
A living tide of green,
Where I, a child,
Barefooted on the clear sand,
Saw the sun fall
Straight and sharp in air—
I screamed in sunrise
As the mare spun
Knee-high
In yellow flowers.

The stones
That held the hills,
The sun that held the
Sky with all its
Spreading rays, were of one
Substance

                and my God
Lay at my feet
And spoke from out
My shadow, eyed me
From the bees:
And he was not, or
Else I—none could
Say.

The Chinamen
Amid the lemongrove
Lived with pale women
And ate dogs and sang
All night.

What wonder, then,
That I went mad
Amid the cloudy stone
And looked at
Print

more beautiful
Than women, till
The earth took form
In my place
at my feet.

IX. *The Moonlight*

I waited on,
In the late autumn moonlight,
A train droning out of thought—

The mind on moonlight
And on trains

Blind as a thread of water
Stirring through a cold like dust,
Lonely beyond all silence,

And humming this to children,
The nostalgic listeners in sleep,

Because no guardian
Strides through distance upon distance,
His eyes a web of sleep.

X. *October*

The houses
Are more bare
And nothing
Dims the hills.

October
Comes and goes
And in the moonlight
I wait for winter.

The silence
Is like moonlight
In one thing:
That it hides nothing.

XI. *The Impalpable Void*

Thinner than Adam who trod
In the garden,
This young man
Bending alone.

Leaves golden as eyes
But no beast comes
Golden and silent,
A rest for the hand.

Scattered autumn—
The leaves will be fainter than rain
Ere he senses the void
High on air

And his vision
Drifts from the place
Where the lawn was,
Where dew was the sea.

XII. *'The Fragile Season'*

The scent of summer thins,
The air grows cold.

One walks alone
And chafes his hands.

The fainter aspens
Thin to air—
                    The dawn
Is frost on roads.

This ending of the year
Is like the lacy ending
        of a last year's leaf
Turned up in silence.

Air gives way to cold.

II. THE BARE HILLS

Sennor, de aquesta coyta saca al
tu arcipreste . . .

I. *Genesis*

The door became a species of mystery.

It opened inward or stood closed.

It was the twofaced god that was able to learn
nothing, save its own reversible path.

II. *Exodus*

Man walks with an unshaken certitude,
pursuing the slow monsters of the brain
through Time's compression of the solitude.

III. *The Vigil*

These were the moments saved from sleep.

The wrinkled tree lay bare along the roof—

death and rebirth of an abstract inertia,
creaking still against the years.

IV. *Moonrise*

The branches,
jointed, pointing
up and out, shine
out like brass.

Upon the heavy
lip of earth
the dog

at
moments is
possessed and screams:

The rising moon draws
up his blood and hair.

V. *Alba for Hecate*

Come down at last
in icy hair of sleep

repeat your
syllables to stone

the dog is shaken

it is spring
upon the cornices

recall the shrunken
petals and the eyelids

of the dog—they
dropped alike

in blinded flight

II. *Digue Dondaine, Digue Dondon*

Sun on the sidewalk
for the corpse to
pass through like the
dark side of a leaf

in the immobile
suddenness of spring
he stood there
in the streetlight
casting a long shadow
on the glassed begonias
madness under
his streaked eyelids

miles away the
cold plow in veined earth

the wind fled hovering
like swarming bees
in highest night

the streets paved with
the moon smooth to
the heels

and he whirled off in

Time

and pale and small
children that run shrieking
through March doorways
burst like bubbles
on the cold twigs
block on block away

I. *March Dusk*

Still I plunge over
rocky mud with
only one thought—
of a naked girl
beneath black eaves
that thunder
in the rain
like risen wings.
The dogs are barking
horribly; and now and
then a gust of
cold rain hovers
in the air and
breaks, and drenches
shoulders, hair, and
legs. Above, the
red cliffs darkening
and filling all
the sky. And under
foot the spring
goes cold and
breathes a lace of
icy foam, shakes
through the earth.

II. *The Lamplight*

Upon the floor the
light like oil but
cloudy in the
air with massy
dark. Your naked
shoulder's splendor.
And I watched you.
Love without a

breath, impassive like
no wine man ever
knew but drawing
passion from my very
flesh. Amid a
scrawl of wood and
stony earth. The night
stood irondomed
above the floor.

III. *Flesh of Flowers*

Beneath
the flinty
pines

that flickered
like a
sleepless eye

your body
bare
alive

on slowveined
feet
that trod

the swollen floor

IV. *Under Rain*

The wind is
pushing like a
great hand
on the steep roof
and the house
sags pressing
water from the turf.

Your deep thighs,
heavy with white,
wade toward me—
and the mind thins in a
wave that
floods the edge of Time.

V. *Midnight Wind*

I pressed you
into place with
cold hands, paused
upon the threshold,
and went down the road.

The wind came
down the gulley
buffeting the earth like a
great rock—

I
trembled in the wind
but found my door
and climbed the stairway
as a man
climbs out of sleep.

And it was not that
I did not believe in
God, but that the quiet
of the room was more
immediate—

it was the
brute passivity
of rough dark wood
beneath my bare feet
where no wind dared
fan the naked fact.

I. *Complaint*

A few leaves red with
rising moon and

here and there a
mandoline cries out

that love is vain

those naked
strings

whip in and out of
mind

lash of the moon

in glowing leaves
like flesh on air

II. *The Muezzin*

The newspaper
hurled
into swarming clouds
returns
cobwebbed with pale beatitude
a certainty of evening

night is
darkening in ripple
over ripple over
stony leaves

                    with
happy eyes I search this
earth of gardens dark as
open doors

to what
obliquity of nothing
do I go
veined cloud O pillared omen

dazed and shrill
the whitelipped boy
now faces the red sun
and cries the news

V. *Song*

Now the precise, remote, and
striking coolness of
fine wood is in the air
sunrise is set as if
reflected from a
violin hung in the
trees—the birds are
lost in admiration in a
stiff wild hall of light

And I preach to them of
the mystery of this my
sacred craft but no one
listens

I a poet
stand about the streets
alive for any audience
and shivering at quiet
as at pure thin morning

I. *Full Moon*

Fair moon, I climb your tide.

II. *Love Song*

What have I said of thee?

III. *Sleep*

O living pine, be still!

II. *The Bare Hills*

Contracted mass—
he struggled
through this
breathing heavily;
it was an absolute,
some grating horror,
spined with rigid age.
And he emerged
into the diningroom
with redveined eyes
that guttered
into sleep.
And he sat down
and ate the bread
as if he ate rock,
while he ground
his buttocks.
He got up and smiled
and went upstairs
to meet the monstrous
nakedness of
his own face
with unchanged step.

III. *The Dead: Mazda Wake*

Hard chair and table
skeleton of feelings
carved away by glassy light

condensed in
grief the old man
walks beside the bed or
lifts the flamepure sheet

to see this
woman: jagged grip on Space

deposited by life
a thought made visible
in wrinkle upon wrinkle
not to be forgotten

but now done and gritty
gathered at his feet.

V. *The Grosbeaks*

The beauty of
these hard
small birds is
clean as scattered seed–
dry penguins
of the cliffs of light!

Along crushed hills
they flutter watching men
who drag the earth
and lengthen
into wrinkles
above thickening frost.

They leap into
the air and
gather,
the blown chaff of
stony ground, and
so are gone.

I. *The Streets*

The algebra of miracles, that
cold that stills the bone to rigid
shadow set in air; the winter sun
which stirs so slowly that it draws the
dim sky with it.

Then one budges from
his door like a deliberate word.
I met the Christ—we quarreled
over sins in various seasons and the venial
pulchritudes, and I consigned him to the flame;
his only answer was that one elegiac smile—
he granted nothing; but at last
we settled it like gentlemen and
walked away; fastidiousness had
filled us as delight a shining flower.

And now the trees burst into light, the
streets the color of the flicker of the
steady feet alike deliberate in swiftness
in a world of vigor where I speak to
one beneath a rigid violence of
sun in leaves and pass along—
the wilderness, inveterate and
slow, a vastness one has
never seen, stings to the tongue and
ear. The terror in the taste
and sound of the unseen has
overwhelmed me; I am on the
mythical and smoky soil at last—

But no: it is
another matter here; the ice becomes
embedded beneath shingles; and, between the
seasons, one is stricken with his consciousness
of cold and his stupidity; trapped and morose.
I met God in the streetcar, but I could not
pray to him, and we were both

embarrassed; and to get away I chose
the first finality—black streets like
unlit windows, coffee hour by hour,
and chilling sleep.

III. *Prayer Beside a Lamp*

'Vasti quoque rector Olympi . . .
Non agat hos currus.'

I pace beside my books and hear the
wind stop short against the house like
a pneumatic gasp of death.
The mind that lives on
print becomes too savage: print that
stings and shivers in the cold when
shingles rise and fall. O God,
my house is built of bone that bends.

Beyond the roof
the sky turns with an endless roaring and bears all
the stars. What could you do?
Could you climb up against the whirling
poles alone? Grind through the ghastly
twist of the sphere? Could you maintain
a foothold on the rising earth for
night on night and walk the
creaking floor?

The steady courage
of the humming oil drives back the
darkness as I drive back sweating death;
from out a body stricken by this thought, I
watch the night grow turgid on the stair—
I, crumbling, in the crumbling brain of man.

IV. *Man Regards Eternity in Aging*

Now rotting Time again leaves bare the god.
The shadowless, august, the spiritless
and changing pines are over him; the hairy cows,
like pinecones, common, roughtongued–
like the wild seeds fallen
from what has been–these move here and there
with caution before earth inert or living.

The dull pines hover with a
motion of the blood.

                    Youth of the village, glassyeyed,
and coated like a dim, unfinished volume in the rain,
the haunter of the rigid silences,
have I apologized?

                    The rough soil
is without depth, shadow, distance; and he
lies there in harshcolored air, breathing, alone.

III. THE PASSING NIGHT

Rey velho que Deus confonda . . .

I. *Eternity*

The small schoolroom was upstairs, and from the narrow windows I could see the hills. The schoolyard was bare, with a few cinderpiles, and the leaves had already fallen from the trees.

The days were gray and still, and the camp was silent. The shacks were dull blue, gray, and brown, and most of them had been there forty years. Back of the main street their arrangement was indefinite.

For days there was no change, and then the snow fell. Change was an abstraction on the air. We were more than ever shut in.

I sat at my desk, barely conscious of the class. My knowing dimmed their brains, and they watched the soundless air secretly.

Sometimes one whispered, and I slapped his hand with a ruler. The hand of a certain negro boy was gray and wrinkled, and curled slowly as the ruler left it; and his mouth widened and contracted a little, slowly, like the hand.

I had seen this boy often, for every evening he hunched close to the stove while the men were eating; and after supper he gathered up what laundry he could, looked at the men with his meaningless smile, and stepped carefully into the winter night. Then I withdrew to an empty room I shared with an indeterminate consciousness. There was no heat, and the soiled blankets were thin.

I did not believe in the existence of precisions. It was no matter whether I sat behind my desk or behind the window of my room. Often I heard the pale Slavs stamping and shouting below me, and one night a man wept with drunkenness.

The cinders in the moonlight were the same: I saw nothing but perpetuity.

II. *The Passing Night*

The oil lamp flamed quietly and darkly: I sat waiting. The old bitch labored amid heavy sighs. On the rough mud of the wall, a bedbug in a haze of wisdom. Shy as a terrapin in spotted light.

I sat on mercilessly into night. I remembered rooms where I had spent the night in spring. Strange railroad stations with an oil lamp near the ceiling. And the stove that no one cares for. One cannot read there. The lamp is low and cold. The claylimbed Mexican across the room is rough with smoke and sleep. In that he is like the walls.

And the hotels with sagging floors and long papery lace curtains swaying in the dark, and decaying wood that has absorbed the odor of innumerable men. I have always come to these rooms late at night and left at dawn. I have always been unutterably sorry for the men I have passed in the corridors, yet I have seldom spoken to them—perhaps because when two men pass each other in a corridor a few hours before dawn, they look straight ahead as if they had seen no one.

Night. Night the terrible. Where niggers die unseen and sink like stones.

The great bitch labored dully, bearing shuddering pools of blackness, one by one.

The lamp was graying in its harsh smoke when I dozed. It was the slopping of the bitch's tongue that awakened me, and light lay on the floor like a swarm of bees.

FOUR POEMS PREVIOUSLY UNCOLLECTED FROM MAGAZINES

THE MULE CORRAL

One mule
Amid the snow
Forever
Turned his head.

The window,
Edged with frost,

Contained
The mule,
A thought
Of autumn,

Uneasy
As a leaf
In endless
Air and snow.

The Milwaukee Arts Monthly, October 1922

THE SCHOOLMASTER AT SPRING

By light blue porches
Flowers are dry
And close to earth,
Like stone
Unmoved by wind.

I think of Santa Cruz—
The bare trees
Like brown earth,
The coming summer,
And the roads
Deep, deep in leaves;
But get no further.
For my books
Like colored stones
Are hard to move;
And I beside them,
A strange man's portrait
On my wall in summer,
Look one way.

Poetry: A Magazine of Verse, May 1923

THE SOLITUDE OF GLASS

No ferns, but
Fringed rock
Spreads on hills
To cover us.

On stone of pollen
At the bend of sight
Stiff rocks
Cast violet eyes

Like rays of shadow,
Roam
Impenetrable
In a cold of glass—

The sun, a lichen
Spreading on the sky
For days
Behind the cold;

The burros,
Like iron-filings
Gathered to
The adamant.

Poetry: A Magazine of Verse, January 1925

PRIMAVERA

Atoms seethe into
the sun it is

the solid
whirling of the

sun itself the
chlorophyl booms

and the chosen race
accelerates the night

of intricate solidity
of splintered pinnacles

against a shivered
heaven whining death

the pavement
heaves in labor and a

goat is born
alive and perfect

and the foam still
clinging to his beard

1924, Number 3.

FIRE SEQUENCE
from *The American Caravan*, 1927

I. *Coal: Beginning and End*

Below the pressure
of the years
what is this
bring it warmth
the writhing heat
without a roothold
yet drives
downward
atom after atom
bounds away
they go

a milky way of spermy slow
explosions over night

2. *Liberation*

My room is bare
come in you
freed from death
now twisting a
slow course in Time
speak to me here
before Time grips us
death is
long—no man may
come to free us—
then your lips
your thighs that seethe interminably.
So evade the years.

3. *Return of Spring*

Spring. The drifting men. The valleys fill.
Gasoline lamps in spring nights—the dances
dripping blood.

The rails beside the station platform are a
watery green. No matter where one turns the
world is difficult to remember. The ticking
from the station starts intermittently.

This only I can never forget: the shrieking
steel amid the wilderness of spring.

I am living in a frame house, empty, gaunt as
an October night, and I am standing in the door.
The dawn clings to the river like a fog. It rises.
I am cold.

Below me are the dried shacks, painted blue,
against electric lights, between the hills. As
cold as a whore's fingers stiff at dawn. Or like
the stones lost in the valley.

4. *Bill*

Come sit here let's
get a room I'm
drunk we got a
room the girl's gone
home
            damn town I
could have killed them
but them four guys
jumped on top of
me with hobnails
caulked their boots to
get the floor they
got my head
                                   the
monkey chased their
mother and the monkey
won
                        but christ
if I was big as
you I'd lick the
world you must be
sweet as hell

look out the window
them damn goats
that sister
sitting down to pee

good kid she was
god! give me air

5. The Vanquished

Alert and bitter in
this blackened time
this light of autumn
streaked with early
winter

I go up the steps
the yellow window
smears black earth
with gold

damned in the heavy
wind smoke earthy
night the house weaves to the
sailing cry black nigger
monkeyface I'll knock you
dead damn I'm as
good as you sunk
toward me in the dark his
breath was steam
I'll - - - - the dirty Slav to death

stiff ruts lay black and heavy
Christ lay
drunk among them in a
gully stones were white in dark He
shuddered into sleep.

6. *The Victor*

The Slav stood in the
door the green light hung a
mist about his black hair
forehead shadowed like the hills
above the valley

the blue hills
the nightfilled
whorl and stone
an element
of some profound
of thought

the hills
in this existence
are an image
for the drowned

can't find my way
the earth is shallow
and I stumble
grasses whip in night
the air like ether
and their blades but names

7. *A Miner*

Dust unto dust and
bone unto the rock
you split the rock it
closed—your brain
flashed out in smoke

now let the granite
press you into
coal black rich
with heat

                    you
warm my heart
great Slav who
stamped and roared
through winter nights
on fragile floors

no plank was made
for you alive or dead
but rock!

                    The wind
shakes riveted
to earth as if you
set your great feet
slowly to its roar

8. *Vacant Lot*

Tough hair like dead
grass over new and
hooves quick and
impatient the he-goat
looks round him
over frozen mud

but
finds no mate

hardeyed
and savage he
turns back and nips
the bitter grass

9. *Tragic Love*

I

The girl went out
and died amid a
cold that clung
like flame.

The God
was gone, but he
came back amid
great splendor
and great heat
and leaves like shells
broke from the
earth and rang in
the thin air
about her black thighs
where no God had been
peering for this
stiff beauty under
cold invisible and
visible—periphery
of air and
globe of winter.

II

Then between her thighs
the seeded grass
of airy summer—
the slow hairlike flame.

10. *To the Crucified*

Alone you fire on
wood cling to the
surface twine about
the cross

it is broad day
the fire is
small and hard and
far away you
are too small

by night you
shrink and gather
and lick into black
I read my paper
by your glare

three nights in hell
you flame of solid gold
rolled over all the surface
lifted atom
after atom

and burst through all Space

but left this fine
incredible and slowly
rushing wake of sound.

11. *O Sun!*

O Sun who make
the earth sweat
shadowy and acid
life for whom the
black pines grip
and tear the living
rock

                        strike
through my body
now I walk alone
to try the depth of earth

red carrots tremble
in a rigid shoal, and
man leaps out
creator of bent Power
blackthrobbing blasphemies

in guts of iron
he mixes stone and
air bricks climb
the trellises of light

great cabbages
roll from the dark
and break choked
black with life

12. *November*

The season roaring
low along the ground
piles up in heavy
swells on throbbing timbers
breaks, a crest of
sound, electric foam that
runs upon the air

on black root-tortured
fields cut into by
white rock

                    the house
the shaken wood
hardrooted in the
cold waits I am strong

come to my room
the stove is iron
I took the hot
dark from the earth
to wrap about you

your grave body
growing in the heart of
wood while the black
season beats the timbers
with its heavy cries

13. *Genesis*

Locked drab and sudden
underfoot the earth is
fierce in silence
forces without Time or
Space have snapped
together and the thing
is wintergray and hard
and without love or change

one gave and I was born
I the slow difference
increase and shrink
and now shall vanish
here and there
a flower is oozing agony
torn between earth and
light: thin flower of Force
it wrinkles gathers bends

no shoulders break this
crystallized electric hatred
bitter with no sense
it is a dream
locked into Time
a dream that bent my brain
that slow vibration
singing out of sound

14. *The Bitter Moon*

Dry snow runs burning
on the ground like fire—
the quick of Hell spin on
the wind. Should I believe
in this your body, take it
at its word? I have believed
in nothing. Earth burns with a
shadow that has held my
flesh; the eye is a shadow
that consumes the mind

Scream into air. The voices
of the dead still vibrate—
they will find them, threading
all the past with twinging
wires alive like hair in cold.
These are the nerves
of death. I am its brain.

You are the way, the oath
I take. I hold to this—
I, bent and thwarted by a will
to live among the living dead
instead of the dead living; I,
become a voice to sound for.
Can you feel through Space,
imagine beyond Time?

The
snow alive with moonlight
licks about my ankles.
Can you find this end?

15. *The Deep: A Service for All the Dead*

Old concentrate of thought, ironveined and slow,
that willed itself and labored out of earth,
man grinds his plow through corrugated rock
and draws a wake that lasts a thousand years:
it thins and gathers, creeps up to the spot
where the brain vanished.

Vanished in concentration,
shrank till he could not stir—
a thought worn small with use, a formula,
a motion, then a stasis, and then nothing.
And in the bent heart of the seething rock
slow crystals shiver, the fine cry of Time.

THE RED MONTH

The passions of
the race are now
embedded in
the air more
fearful in their
pride of silence
moving rapidly afar
as changes of
the hour or as a
month across the grass

now incest burns
the very shade
hate rains about me
in the red light
through the trees

July! a bird drops
to the sidewalk
like a stone.

INCANDESCENT EARTH

Hills red and brown
and matted
springy with scruboak
the dust and sagesmell
heat
a stifling cloud
rose at the touch
leaves fell to ash

more heat beat from
the earth
than from the sun the
rock
was hot all night

the coral snakes
flowed
rolling over smoking rock
in sluggish agony
in search of sleep

ORANGE TREE

Hard, oily,
sinuous,
your trunk,

black serpent,
struggling
with your weight of gold—

great strength
massed
against Time,

in angry pride
you hold out
lacquered life

the classic leaf.

SEE LOS ANGELES FIRST

Rosyfingered cocklehouses
burst from burning
rock red plaster hollyhocks
spit crackling mamas
tickled pink

on tiptoe
yawn into the dewy dawn
dark wettish plushy lawn

MIZPAH
The Temple glittergates
Ask God He Knows
O pyramid of Sunoil Dates

The mockingbird is singing
eighty languages a minute
swinging by his toes from
highpower
jagged geometric currents
roar along aluminum gashed
out of gulleys rending
night to one blind
halo for your cold

concrete Egyptian nakedness
O watertower of cleanliness

TO THE PAINTER POLELONEMA

You wring life
from the rock
from gold air
violent with odors
smoking wrath

you seize life
in the naked hand
crush, smelt it,
temper–
in a single grip
that lasts for years

it is
for this one lives

and drives a
brain into the rock
and bursts the veins
with love–
                    of rock!

No sparrow
cracks these seeds

that no wind blows.

BISON

O eye of grief
O fire of hairy
earth

          gunpowder
of the beating
rock!

          You
clove the silence
stared into the sun
O bed of burning
horns

          O swarming
blood that stored black
honey in your flesh

thighed with the storm!

REMEMBERED SPRING

Sweet, hard, and swift the Spring
comes up those mountains,
clusters, bending on bare branches–
every leaf is stinging with new life!

Give me your hand–
flesh sweetens on that cliff
like winter apples. Wood
holds the air still, crisp
against hail, against electric
apertures to Hell!

                    The naked
buds exploded into life
from out of naked space–
no starting point, no end.

                    I found that Spring
in early March, six inches
under ground. Soaked,
swollen hard with water,
violent with meaning!

Living beauty, eating with the eyes,
by my eyes eaten! I burned into all,
stained, staining, in three colors,
hard with joy!

WILD SUNFLOWER

Sunflower! gross of leaf and porous,
gummy, raw,
with unclean edges,

fury
of the broken but unbeaten
earth, it leers
beside our door!

Grip
hard to the dry
airy logs, scoured
clean with sun. Hold fast
to what you are, in spite of
the wormseething loam,
the boiling land. And give
me love, slow love
that draws the turgid
loam up into sun!

But
fiercely this thing
grows, is hairy, is
unfinished at the edges,
gulps the sun and earth, will
not be beaten
down nor turn away.

SATYRIC COMPLAINT

The water burning through the
flesh has left it worn thin
stretched and sunken
dog exhausted drops head
on dark paws the
dog magnificent in May!
head up against hard
slowly splitting buds!

While
underground flowers icy-veined bud
break forth and look back to
seek an image in an element
too still for them too certain.

So
have I been. Born
to die for man. Born to believe, to
be believed. Dark scent of earth
crushed in the hand. Thighskin of hairy
bark. The earth became wood, wood was
flesh, flesh beauty, beauty mind. Mind
became agony to glare
from gray eyes knowing
its end rooted in its feet.

Wood broken by new light. Dogteeth
of dawn. I live and
suffer, twist rootfooted from black
street to street, blurred in the brain.

Blunt boats all night
groan against granite surge. Wet
wind strikes solid on
the flesh the cry starts
from the heels, on concrete,
shatters living bone.

THE LONGE NIGHTES WHEN EVERY CREATURE . . .

Through the long
winter nights when every
beast turns steaming
in his sleep
I lie alone an eddy
fixed, alive with
change that is not I:
slow torture
this to lie and hold
to mind against the stream
with nought
to seize on: the bed trembles
to my blood. I break
the night, I break
the soundless flow, I
cry and turn and the cold
gathers round my hands
and thickened brain:
a girl lay naked
in my bed
with cold small arms
and wept. The humming tongue
burrows the nightwind
of the nightingale
that comes no more.

SNOW-GHOST

Bleak air a fear
a dreaming monster turning
slowly that will
flake away

                    in hollow gloam
age spiralling in Time

Draw back

the shining blind
the vibrant membrane
singing back a
dream

              come to me
where I stand O
where I sifting change

invisible save on this plane of light

I look both ways and wait

Behind the window, waterclear
volcanic trees of winter
against crumbling sky

SONNET

The table softly flames with flowers and candles
flame in wax and wax in flame and flame in flesh
and flaming flesh in silver
and your hand draws fruit from air

grown substance. And beyond the pane
moonlight is eating into earth—where the night
glimmers. My eyes will not rest.
We lose reality in symbolism,

stripped of our own meaning,
simplified for men. Beyond elision,
tragic if displaced! God stalks

in my living hand the mind,
the prey equivocal. The mind escapes.
You, set before me on a shaft of night!

THE VIGIL

To grind out bread by facing God!
The elbows, bone wedged
into wood with stubborn grief; the hard face
gripping the mad night in the vision's vise.

The floor burns underfoot, atomic
flickering to feigned rigidity: God's
fierce derision, and outside the oak
is living slowly but is strong; it grips
a moment to a thousand years; and it
will move across our gasping
bodies in the end.

This is no
place to wait out Time. To see you
strikes my heart with terror,
speeding Time to violence and death.

The thought, the leap, is measured: madness
will return to sanity. The pendulum. Here.
Trapped in Time.

STRENGTH OUT OF SWEETNESS

Three nights I sat beside
your bier with two old women,
graying grimaces
now stiffening toward death–
I, cold with grief.

They drew the curtains
back to let me see–
it struck me
dumb that I should know you.

Your two sons
stood there with forearms
great
from tearing at the rooted
hills. They could not see.

But I
had known; had passed
your chair and had not
paused to speak–your face
aflow with agony. Now stopped.

And basic, clear. All
had passed over it. And this
lay bare: rock
rigid unto God.

I stood unseen.

SIMPLEX MUNDITIIS

The goat nips yellow blossoms
shaken loose from rain—
with neck extended
lifts a twitching flower
high into wet air. Hard
humility the lot of man
to crouch beside
this creature in the dusk
and hold the mind clear;
to turn the sod,
to face the sod beside his door,
to wound it as his own flesh.
In the spring the blossoms
drown the air with joy,
the heart with sorrow.
One must think of this
in quiet. One must
bow his head and take
with roughened hands
sweet milk at dusk,
the classic gift of earth.

II / COLLECTED POEMS

To Professor and Mrs Richard Foster Jones
with admiration and affection

NOTE: The title *Collected Poems* may seem too ambitious for this volume;* for the volume is not a complete collection of what I have published by a very wide margin. However, the volume contains everything which I wish to keep and represents in addition a kind of definition by example of the style which I have been trying to achieve for a matter of thirty years. The poems omitted seem to me inferior in quality, and they would certainly obscure the issue which for me is the principal issue.

Y. W.

*This note was written for *Collected Poems* (Alan Swallow, 1960).

A SONG OF ADVENT

On the desert, between pale mountains, our cries:
Far whispers creeping through an ancient shell.

SONG

I could tell
Of silence where
One ran before
Himself and fell
Into silence
Yet more fair.

TO BE SUNG BY A SMALL BOY WHO HERDS GOATS

Sweeter than rough hair
On earth there is none:
Rough as the wind
And brown as the sun!

I toss high my short arms,
Brown as the sun!
I creep on the mountains
And never am done!

Sharp-hoofed, hard-eyed,
Trample on the sun!
Sharp ears, stiff as wind,
Point the way to run!

Who on the brown earth
Knows himself one?
Life is in lichens
That sleep as they run.

ALONE

I, one who never speaks,
Listened days in summer trees,
Each day a rustling leaf!
Then, in time, my unbelief
Grew like my running:
My own eyes did not exist!
When I struck I never missed!
Noon, felt and far away,
My brain is a thousand bees.

THE LIE

I paved a sky
   With days.
I crept beyond the Lie.
   This phrase,
Yet more profound,
   Grew where
I was not. I
   Was there.

NOON

Did you move, in the sun?

THE SHADOW'S SONG

I am beside you, now.

THE ASPEN'S SONG

The summer holds me here.

GOD OF ROADS

I, peregrine of noon.

SLEEP

O living pine, be still!

THE PRECINCTS OF FEBRUARY

Junipers,
Steely shadows,
Floating the jay.
A man,

Heavy and iron-black,
Alone in sun,
Threading the grass.
The cold,

Coming again
As Spring
Came up the valley,
But to stay

Rooted deep in the land.
The stone-pierced shadows
Trod by the bird
For day on day.

JOSE'S COUNTRY

A pale horse,
Mane of flowery dust,
Runs too far for a sound
To cross the river.

Afternoon,
Swept by far hooves
That gleam
Like slow fruit
Falling
In the haze
Of pondered vision.

It is nothing.
Afternoon
Beyond a child's thought,
Where a falling stone
Would raise pale earth,
A fern ascending.

THE UPPER MEADOWS

The harvest falls
Throughout the valleys
With a sound
Of fire in leaves.

The harsh trees,
Heavy with light,
Beneath the flame, and aging,
Have risen high and higher.

Apricots,
The clustered
Fur of bees
Above the gray rocks of the uplands.

The hunter deep in summer.
Grass laid low by what comes,
Feet or air—
But motion, aging.

THE GOATHERDS

The trees are
the rayed pillars
of the sun where
small boys gather
seashells in the desert;
goats move here and there;
the small boys
shriek amid white rocks,
run at the river;
and the sky has
risen in red dust
and stricken
villages with distance
till the brown feet quiver
on the rock like
fallen eyelids and the
goat's hoof, tiny,
jet, is like a twig about
to burst in flame.

And then
the motion once again like
tiny blossoms
far away beside the river
and the cries of
small boys like the
cries of birds at dawn.

SONG OF THE TREES

Belief is blind! Bees scream!
Gongs! Thronged with light!

                    And I take
into light, hold light,
in light I live, I,
pooled and broken here,
to watch, to wake above you.

                    Sun,
no seeming, but savage
simplicity, breaks running
for an aeon, stops, shuddering, here.

THE COLD

Frigidity the hesitant
uncurls its tentacles
into a furry sun.
The ice expands
into an insecurity
that should appal
yet I remain
astray in this
oblivion, this
inert labyrinth
of sentences that
dare not end. It
is high noon and
all is the more quiet
where I trace
the courses of the Crab
and Scorpion, the Bull,
the Hunter, and the Bear—
with front of steel
they cut an aperture
so clear across the
cold that it cannot
be seen: there is no
smoky breath, no
breath at all.

QUOD TEGIT OMNIA

Earth darkens and is beaded
with a sweat of bushes and
the bear comes forth;
the mind, stored with
magnificence, proceeds into
the mystery of time, now
certain of its choice of
passion, but uncertain of the
passion's end.

When
Plato temporizes on the nature
of the plumage of the soul the
wind hums in the feathers as
across a cord impeccable in
tautness but of no mind:

Time,
the sine-pondere, most
imperturbable of elements,
assumes its own proportions
silently, of its own properties—
an excellence at which one
sighs.

Adventurer in
living fact, the poet
mounts into the spring,
upon his tongue the taste of
air becoming body: is
embedded in this crystalline
precipitate of time.

NOCTURNE

Moonlight on stubbleshining hills
whirls down upon me finer than geometry
and at my very
face it blurs and softens like a dream

In leafblack houses
linen smooth with sleep
and folded by cold life itself for limbs so definite

their passion is
persistent like a pane of glass

about their feet the clustered
birds are sleeping
heavy with incessant life

The dogs swim close to earth

A kildee rises
dazed and rolled amid the sudden blur of sleep
above the dayglare of the fields
goes screaming
off toward darker hills

SONG

Where I walk out
to meet you on the
cloth of burning
fields

the goldfinches
leap up about my
feet like angry
dandelions

quiver like a
heartbeat in the
air and are
no more

APRIL

The little goat
crops
new grass lying down
leaps up eight inches
into air and
lands on four feet.
Not a tremor—
solid in the
spring and serious
he walks away.

THE COLD ROOM

The dream
stands
in the night
above unpainted
floor and chair.

The dog is
dead asleep
and
will not move
for god or fire.

And from the
ceiling
darkness bends
a heavy flame.

THE BARNYARD

The wind appears
and disappears
like breath on a mirror
and between the hills
is only cold
that lies
beneath the stones
and in the grass.
The sleeping dog
becomes a
knot of twinging turf.
It was the
spring that left
this rubbish
and these scavengers
for ice to kill—
this old man
wrinkled in
the fear of Hell, the
child that staggers
straight into
the clotting cold
with short fierce cries.

THE ROWS OF COLD TREES

To be my own Messiah to the
burning end. Can one endure the
acrid, steeping darkness of
the brain, which glitters and is
dissipated? Night. The night is
winter and a dull man bending,
muttering above a freezing pipe;
and I, bent heavily on books; the
mountain, iron in my sleep and
ringing; but the pipe has frozen, haired with
unseen veins, and cold is on the eyelids: who can
remedy this vision?

I have walked upon
the streets between the trees that
grew unleaved from asphalt in a night of
sweating winter in distracted silence.

I have
walked among the tombs—the rushing of the air
in the rich pines above my head is that which
ceaseth not nor stirreth whence it is:
in this the sound of wind is like a flame.

It was the dumb decision of the
madness of my youth that left me with
this cold eye for the fact; that keeps me
quiet, walking toward a
stinging end: I am alone,
and, like the alligator cleaving timeless mud,
among the blessed who have Latin names.

THE LADY'S FAREWELL

from the thirteenth century Galician

Awake, my love, who sleep into the dawn!
The birds of all the world cried and are gone.
I go away in joy.

Awake, my love, who sleep so late at dawn!
It was our love the small birds dwelt upon.
I go away in joy.

The birds of all the world spoke of our love,
Of my love and of yours cried out above.
I go away in joy.

The birds of all the world sang loud at day.
It was my love and yours, I heard them say.
I go away in joy.

It was my love and yours that made their song.
You cut the branches where they clung so long.
I go away in joy.

It was my love and yours that made their cry—
You cut the branches where they used to fly.
I go away in joy.

You cut the branches where they used to sing,
And where they came to drink you dried the spring.
I go away in joy.

You cut the branches where they used to stay,
And dried the waters where they came to play.
I go away in joy.

—Nuño Fernández Torneol

COSSANTE

from the thirteenth century Galician

Tell me, daughter, my pretty daughter,
Why you waited by the cold water.
—It was love, alas!

Tell me, daughter, my lovely daughter,
Why you waited by the cold water.
—It was love, alas!

I waited, mother, by the cold fountain
While the deer came down the mountain.
—It was love, alas!

I waited by the cold river, mother,
To see the deer, and not for any other.
—It was love, alas!

You lie, daughter, you lie for your lover,
I never saw deer come down from cover.
—It was love, alas!

You lie, daughter, for your lover by the fountain,
I never saw deer going up to the mountain.
—It was love, alas!

—Pero Meogo

POEM

from the sixteenth century Spanish

Nothing move thee;
Nothing terrify thee;
Everything passes;
God never changes.
Patience be all to thee.
Who trusts in God, he
Never shall be needy.
God alone suffices.

—Saint Theresa

DEATH'S WARNINGS

from the seventeenth century Spanish

I looked upon the old walls of my land—
Once they were strong, and now they fall away.
Tired with the march of age, they may not stay—
Their strength has vanished, and they scarcely stand.
I went out to the fields, and from the sand
The sun drank up the brooks that broke to play
And drank the crying flocks that stole the day
From off the mountain with their shadowy band.

I went into my house, and there I found
The rotted leavings of an ancient race:
I found my staff more twisted and less sound,
I felt my sword that crumbled at the breath
Of age, and saw no thing in all the place
That did not seem an harbinger of death.

—Francisco de Quevedo y Villegas

CANTABRIA

from the nineteenth century Spanish

Agëd orchards, gently flowing
Waters of the clearest fountains,
Thin air of the higher mountains,
Little valleys always shining
With white houses and black towers
And the sea forever creeping,
Where the spirit broods in quiet;
Blessëd sweat upon the forehead—
This it is inspires my hours,
And with these Cantabria keeps me.
Should I vanish, let them seek me
From Higuer to Finisterre.

—Antonio de Trueba

ROME

from the sixteenth century French

You, who behold in wonder Rome and all
Her former passion, menacing the gods,
These ancient palaces and baths, the sods
Of seven hills, and temple, arch, and wall,
Consider, in the ruins of her fall,
That which destroying Time has gnawed away—
What workmen built with labor day by day
Only a few worn fragments now recall.

Then look again and see where, endlessly
Treading upon her own antiquity,
Rome has rebuilt herself with works as just:
There you may see the demon of the land
Forcing himself again with fatal hand
To raise the city from this ruined dust.

—Joachim du Bellay

REFLECTIONS

from the seventeenth century French

I

Why rejoice in beauty? What
In all the world is half so vain?
Nay, there is naught
Gives so much pain.
I know that over hearts her rule is sore,
While one is beautiful that she
May have of passion and of lovers store:
But that has little time to be
And a long time to be no more.

II

Pathetic plaything of a witless chance,
Victim of evils and of laws,
Man, who in whatever cause,
Must suffer life's impertinence,
Still, after all that's past,
Whence comes it that you fear the power of death?
Coward! regard it with unhurried breath,
And know this outrage for the last.

—Madame des Houlières

THE SKELETON LABORER

Written to the flayed and fleshless figures on an anatomical chart—from the nineteenth century French

Out of the earth at which you spade,
Funereal laborers, tired and done,
Out of your straining naked bone,
Out of your muscles bare and frayed,

Tell me, what harvest do you win?
Slaves snatched from the charnel ground,
Who is the farmer drives this round
To fill his barn? And what your sin?

You, the terrible sign we're shown
Of our destiny's greater dearth,
Wish you to say that in the earth
The promised sleep is never known?

That the end has betrayed us here,
That even death himself has lied?
That though eternity betide,
Alas! we have again to fear

That in some unknown land we'll meet
A knotted earth that needs be flayed—
To drive again the heavy spade
Beneath our bleeding naked feet?

—Charles Baudelaire

GREEN

from the nineteenth century French

Here you have fruits and flowers and boughs with leaves,
And then my heart, which beats for you alone—
May your white hands not tear it—humble sheaves!
May they seem sweet to you when they are shown!

I come again all covered with the dew
That morning wind has frozen on my brow.
Suffer my weariness, at rest near you,
To dream of quiet that I come to now.

Upon this young breast, let my dull head fall,
Ringing with your last kisses; this, and, best,
Let it grow quiet there from storm and all
In a brief sleep, since you too are at rest.

—Paul Verlaine

A SIGH

from the nineteenth century French

Calm sister, toward your quiet brow where dreams
Roan autumn, toward the questing heaven of
Your eye, my soul mounts steadily; it seems
A jet of water sighing faithfully
Toward heaven in some worn garden; and, above,
October's blue is tender, pale, and pure,
And looks into the fountain with its sure
And infinite languor; in tawn agony
The leaves go with the wind and mark a dun
Hard furrow near a long cold line of sun.

—Stéphane Mallarmé

MARINE

from the nineteenth century French

The chariots of silver and copper,
The prows of steel and of silver,
Beat foam,
Tear up the blackberry stems.

Land-currents,
The immense paths of the reflux,
File in a circle to eastward,
Toward the columns of the forest,
Towards the piles of the jetty,
The angle of which is hit by the whirlwinds of light.

—Arthur Rimbaud

THE MORALISTS

You would extend the mind beyond the act,
Furious, bending, suffering in thin
And unpoetic dicta; you have been
Forced by hypothesis to fiercer fact.
As metal singing hard, with firmness racked,
You formulate our passion; and behind
In some harsh moment nowise of the mind
Lie the old meanings your advance has packed.

No man can hold existence in the head.
I, too, have known the anguish of the right
Amid this net of mathematic dearth,
And the brain throbbing like a ship at night:
Have faced with old unmitigated dread
The hard familiar wrinkles of the earth.

THE REALIZATION

Death. Nothing is simpler. One is dead.
The set face now will fade out; the bare fact,
Related movement, regular, intact,
Is reabsorbed, the clay is on the bed.
The soul is mortal, nothing: the dim head
On the dim pillow, less. But thought clings flat
To this, since it can never follow that
Where no precision of the mind is bred.

Nothing to think of between you and All!
Screaming processionals of infinite
Logic are grinding down receding cold!
O fool! Madness again! Turn not, for it
Lurks in each paintless cranny, and you sprawl
Blurring a definition. Quick! you are old.

TO WILLIAM DINSMORE BRIGGS CONDUCTING HIS SEMINAR

Amid the walls' insensate white, some crime
Is redefined above the sunken mass
Of crumbled years; logic reclaims the crass,
Frees from historic dross the invidious mime.
Your fingers spin the pages into Time;
And in between, moments of darkness pass
Like undiscovered instants in the glass,
Amid the image, where the demons climb.

Climb and regard and mean, yet not emerge.
And in the godless thin electric glare
I watch your face spun momently along
Till the dark moments close and wrinkles verge
On the definitive and final stare:
And that hard book will now contain this wrong.

THE INVADERS

They have won out at last and laid us bare,
The demons of the meaning of the dead,
Stripped us with wheel and flame. Oh, where they tread,
Dissolves our heritage of earth and air!
Till as a locomotive plunges through
Distance that has no meaning and no bound
Thundering some interminable sound
To inward metal where its motion grew—

Grew and contracted down through infinite
And sub-atomic roar of Time on Time
Toward meaning that its changing cannot find;
So, stripped of color of an earth, and lit
With motion only of some inner rime,
The naked passion of the human mind.

TO EMILY DICKINSON

Dear Emily, my tears would burn your page,
But for the fire-dry line that makes them burn—
Burning my eyes, my fingers, while I turn
Singly the words that crease my heart with age.
If I could make some tortured pilgrimage
Through words or Time or the blank pain of Doom
And kneel before you as you found your tomb,
Then I might rise to face my heritage.

Yours was an empty upland solitude
Bleached to the powder of a dying name;
The mind, lost in a word's lost certitude
That faded as the fading footsteps came
To trace an epilogue to words grown odd
In that hard argument which led to God.

THE CASTLE OF THORNS

Through autumn evening, water whirls thin blue,
From iron to iron pail—old, lined, and pure;
Beneath, the iron is indistinct, secure
In revery that cannot reach to you.
Water it was that always lay between
The mind of man and that harsh wall of thorn,
Of stone impenetrable, where the horn
Hung like the key to what it all might mean.

My goats step guardedly, with delicate
Hard flanks and forest hair, unchanged and firm,
A strong tradition that has not grown old.
Peace to the lips that bend in intricate
Old motions, that flinch not before their term!
Peace to the heart that can accept this cold!

APOLLO AND DAPHNE

Deep in the leafy fierceness of the wood,
Sunlight, the cellular and creeping pyre,
Increased more slowly than aetherial fire:
But it increased and touched her where she stood.
The god had seized her, but the powers of good
Struck deep into her veins; with rending flesh
She fled all ways into the grasses' mesh
And burned more quickly than the sunlight could.

And all her heart broke stiff in leafy flame
That neither rose nor fell, but stood aghast;
And she, rooted in Time's slow agony,
Stirred dully, hard-edged laurel, in the past;
And, like a cloud of silence or a name,
The god withdrew into Eternity.

THE FABLE

Beyond the steady rock the steady sea,
In movement more immovable than station,
Gathers and washes and is gone. It comes,
A slow obscure metonymy of motion,
Crumbling the inner barriers of the brain.
But the crossed rock braces the hills and makes
A steady quiet of the steady music,
Massive with peace.

And listen, now:
The foam receding down the sand silvers
Between the grains, thin, pure as virgin words,
Lending a sheen to Nothing, whispering.

THE EMPTY HILLS

Flintridge, Pasadena

The grandeur of deep afternoons,
The pomp of haze on marble hills,
Where every white-walled villa swoons
Through violence that heat fulfills,

Pass tirelessly and more alone
Than kings that time has laid aside.
Safe on their massive sea of stone
The empty tufted gardens ride.

Here is no music, where the air
Drives slowly through the airy leaves.
Meaning is aimless motion where
The sinking hummingbird conceives.

No book nor picture has inlaid
This life with darkened gold, but here
Men passionless and dumb invade
A quiet that entrances fear.

HYMN TO DISPEL HATRED AT MIDNIGHT

Here where I watch the dew
That gathers by the door,
Here where the time is true
   And on the floor
My shadow stirs no more,

The slow night burns away.
Nay, neither I nor Time
Can manage quite to stay—
   We seek a clime
Bound in a moment's chime.

Men are like blades of grass
Beneath a winter sky,
The constellations pass,
   The air is dry
From star to living eye.

Hence unto God, unsought,
My anguish sets. Oh, vain
The heart that hates! Oh, naught
   So drenched in pain!
Grief will not turn again.

MOONRISE

The slow moon draws
The shadows through the leaves.
The change it weaves
Eludes design or pause.

And here we wait
In moon a little space,
And face to face
We know the hour grows late.

We turn from sleep
And hold our breath a while,
As mile on mile
The terror drifts more deep.

So we must part
In ruin utterly—
Reality
Invades the crumbling heart.

We scarce shall weep
For what no change retrieves.
The moon and leaves
Shift here and there toward sleep.

THE FALL OF LEAVES

The green has suddenly
Divided to pure flame,
Leaf-tongued from tree to tree.
Yea, where we stood it came.

This change may have no name,
Yet it was like a word
Spoken, and none to blame,
Alive where shadow stirred.

So was the instant blurred.
But as we waited there,
The slow cry of a bird
Built up a scheme of air.

The vision of despair
Starts at the moment's bound,
Seethes from the vibrant air
With slow autumnal sound

Into the burning ground.

INSCRIPTION FOR A GRAVEYARD

When men are laid away,
Revolving seasons bring
New love, corrupting clay
And hearts dissevering.

Hearts that were once so fast,
Sickened with living blood,
Will rot to change at last.
The dead have hardihood.

Death is Eternity,
And all who come there stay.
For choice, now certainty.
No moment breaks away.

Amid this wilderness,
Dazed in a swarm of hours,–
Birds tangled numberless!–
Archaic Summer towers.

The dead are left alone–
Theirs the intenser cost.
You followed to a stone,
And there the trail was lost.

THE LAST VISIT

For Henry Ahnefeldt, 1862-1929

The drift of leaves grows deep, the grass
Is longer everywhere I pass.
And listen! where the wind is heard,
The surface of the garden's blurred—
It is the passing wilderness.
The garden will be something less
When others win it back from change.
We shall not know it then; a strange
Presence will be musing there.
Ruin has touched familiar air,
And we depart. Where you should be,
I sought a final memory.

FOR HOWARD BAKER

Now autumn's end draws down
Hard twilight by the door;
The wash of rain will drown
Our evening words no more.

Words we have had in store.
But men must move apart
Though what has gone before
Have changed the living heart.

Music and strength of art
Beneath long winter rain
Have played the living part,
With the firm mind for gain.

Nor is the mind in vain.

THE SLOW PACIFIC SWELL

Far out of sight forever stands the sea,
Bounding the land with pale tranquillity.
When a small child, I watched it from a hill
At thirty miles or more. The vision still
Lies in the eye, soft blue and far away:
The rain has washed the dust from April day;
Paint-brush and lupine lie against the ground;
The wind above the hill-top has the sound
Of distant water in unbroken sky;
Dark and precise the little steamers ply—
Firm in direction they seem not to stir.
That is illusion. The artificer
Of quiet, distance holds me in a vise
And holds the ocean steady to my eyes.

Once when I rounded Flattery, the sea
Hove its loose weight like sand to tangle me
Upon the washing deck, to crush the hull;
Subsiding, dragged flesh at the bone. The skull
Felt the retreating wash of dreaming hair.
Half drenched in dissolution, I lay bare.
I scarcely pulled myself erect; I came
Back slowly, slowly knew myself the same.
That was the ocean. From the ship we saw
Gray whales for miles: the long sweep of the jaw,
The blunt head plunging clean above the wave.
And one rose in a tent of sea and gave
A darkening shudder; water fell away;
The whale stood shining, and then sank in spray.

A landsman, I. The sea is but a sound.
I would be near it on a sandy mound,
And hear the steady rushing of the deep
While I lay stinging in the sand with sleep.
I have lived inland long. The land is numb.
It stands beneath the feet, and one may come
Walking securely, till the sea extends

Its limber margin, and precision ends.
By night a chaos of commingling power,
The whole Pacific hovers hour by hour.
The slow Pacific swell stirs on the sand,
Sleeping to sink away, withdrawing land,
Heaving and wrinkled in the moon, and blind;
Or gathers seaward, ebbing out of mind.

THE MARRIAGE

Incarnate for our marriage you appeared,
Flesh living in the spirit and endeared
By minor graces and slow sensual change.
Through every nerve we made our spirits range.
We fed our minds on every mortal thing:
The lacy fronds of carrots in the spring,
Their flesh sweet on the tongue, the salty wine
From bitter grapes, which gathered through the vine
The mineral drouth of autumn concentrate,
Wild spring in dream escaping, the debate
Of flesh and spirit on those vernal nights,
Its resolution in naive delights,
The young kids bleating softly in the rain—
All this to pass, not to return again.
And when I found your flesh did not resist,
It was the living spirit that I kissed,
It was the spirit's change in which I lay:
Thus, mind in mind we waited for the day.
When flesh shall fall away, and, falling, stand
Wrinkling with shadow over face and hand,
Still I shall meet you on the verge of dust
And know you as a faithful vestige must.
And, in commemoration of our lust,
May our heirs seal us in a single urn,
A single spirit never to return.

ON A VIEW OF PASADENA FROM THE HILLS

From the high terrace porch I watch the dawn.
No light appears, though dark has mostly gone,
Sunk from the cold and monstrous stone. The hills
Lie naked but not light. The darkness spills
Down the remoter gulleys; pooled, will stay
Too low to melt, not yet alive with day.
Below the windows, the lawn, matted deep
Under its close-cropped tips with dewy sleep,
Gives off a faint hush, all its plushy swarm
Alive with coolness reaching to be warm.
Gray windows at my back, the massy frame
Dull with the blackness that has not a name;
But down below, the garden is still young,
Of five years' growth, perhaps, and terrace-hung,
Drop by slow drop of seeping concrete walls.
Such are the bastions of our pastorals!

Here are no palms! They once lined country ways,
Where old white houses glared down dusty days,
With small round towers, blunt-headed through small trees.
Those towers are now the hiving place of bees.
The palms were coarse; their leaves hung thick with dust;
The roads were muffled deep. But now deep rust
Has fastened on the wheels that labored then.
Peace to all such, and to all sleeping men!
I lived my childhood there, a passive dream
In the expanse of that recessive scheme.

Slow air, slow fire! O deep delay of Time!
That summer crater smoked like slaking lime,
The hills so dry, so dense the underbrush,
That where I pushed my way the giant hush
Was changed to soft explosion as the sage
Broke down to powdered ash, the sift of age,
And fell along my path, a shadowy rift.

On these rocks now no burning ashes drift;
Mowed lawn has crept along the granite bench;

The yellow blossoms of acacia drench
The dawn with pollen; and, with waxen green,
The long leaves of the eucalypti screen
The closer hills from view—lithe, tall, and fine,
And nobly clad with youth, they bend and shine.
The small dark pool, jutting with living rock,
Trembles at every atmospheric shock,
Blurred to its depth with the cold living ooze.
From cloudy caves, heavy with summer dews,
The shyest and most tremulous beings stir,
The pulsing of their fins a lucent blur,
That, like illusion, glances off the view.
The pulsing mouths, like metronomes, are true.

This is my father's house, no homestead here
That I shall live in, but a shining sphere
Of glass and glassy moments, frail surprise,
My father's phantasy of Paradise;
Which melts upon his death, which he attained
With loss of heart for every step he gained.
Too firmly gentle to displace the great,
He crystallized this vision somewhat late;
Forbidden now to climb the garden stair,
He views the terrace from a window chair.
His friends, hard shaken by some twenty years,
Tremble with palsy and with senile fears,
In their late middle age gone cold and gray.
Fine men, now broken. That the vision stay,
They spend astutely their depleted breath,
With tired ironic faces wait for death.

Below the garden the hills fold away.
Deep in the valley, a mist fine as spray,
Ready to shatter into spinning light,
Conceals the city at the edge of night.
The city, on the tremendous valley floor,
Draws its dream deeper for an instant more,
Superb on solid loam, and breathing deep,
Poised for a moment at the edge of sleep.

Cement roads mark the hills, wide, bending free
Of cliff and headland. Dropping toward the sea,
Through suburb after suburb, vast ravines
Swell to the summer drone of fine machines.
The driver, melting down the distance here,
May cast in flight the faint hoof of a deer
Or pass the faint head set perplexedly.
And man-made stone outgrows the living tree,
And at its rising, air is shaken, men
Are shattered, and the tremor swells again,
Extending to the naked salty shore,
Rank with the sea, which crumbles evermore.

THE JOURNEY

Snake River Country

I now remembered slowly how I came,
I, sometime living, sometime with a name,
Creeping by iron ways across the bare
Wastes of Wyoming, turning in despair,
Changing and turning, till the fall of night,
Then throbbing motionless with iron might.
Four days and nights! Small stations by the way,
Sunk far past midnight! Nothing one can say
Names the compassion they stir in the heart.
Obscure men shift and cry, and we depart.

And I remembered with the early sun
That foul-mouthed barber back in Pendleton,
The sprawling streets, the icy station bench,
The Round-up pennants, the latrinal stench.
These towns are cold by day, the flesh of vice
Raw and decisive, and the will precise;
At night the turbulence of drink and mud,
Blue glare of gas, the dances dripping blood,
Fists thudding murder in the shadowy air,
Exhausted whores, sunk to a changeless stare.
Alive in empty fact alone, extreme,
They make each fact a mortuary dream.

Once when the train paused in an empty place,
I met the unmoved landscape face to face;
Smoothing abysses that no stream could slake,
Deep in its black gulch crept the heavy Snake,
The sound diffused, and so intently firm,
It seemed the silence, having change nor term.
Beyond the river, gray volcanic stone
In rolling hills: the river moved alone.
And when we started, charged with mass, and slow,
We hung against it in an awful flow.

Thus I proceeded until early night,
And, when I read the station's name aright,
Descended—at the bidding of a word!
I slept the night out where the thought occurred,
Then rose to view the dwelling where I lay.
Outside, the bare land stretching far away;
The frame house, new, fortuitous, and bright,
Pointing the presence of the morning light;
A train's far screaming, clean as shining steel
Planing the distance for the gliding heel.
Through shrinking frost, autumnal grass uncurled,
In naked sunlight, on a naked world.

A VISION

Years had elapsed; the long room was the same.
At the far end, a log with drooping flame
Cast lengthening shadow. I was there alone,
A presence merely, like a shadow thrown,
Changing and growing dark with what I knew.
Above the roof, as if through a long flue,
The midnight wind poured steadily through pines.
I saw the trees flame thin, in watery lines.

Then, from my station in the empty air,
I saw them enter by the door; that pair
Opened and closed and watched each other move
With murderous eyes and gestures deep with love.
First came the Widow, but she had no face—
Naught but a shadow. At an earth-soaked pace
Her lover followed, weak with fear and lust.
And then I noticed there were years of dust
On floor and table, thought that in my day
No pines had been there. They sat down to play
At cards on a small table, and made tea,
And ate and played in silence. I could see
His lust come on him slowly, and his head
Fall on the table, but uncomforted
He feared to reach across to find her hand.
Deep in her veil I saw the features stand,
A deep jaw open; and a low iron laugh
Came from afar, a furious epigraph
To what I knew not in another place.
What evil was there in that woman's face!
He shrank in fear and told her of his love,
And she smiled coldly on him from above,
Stooped to a bundle lying by her side
And with a sodden tenderness untied
A severed head, gazed, and denied his plea.
He shuddered, heavy with lubricity.

There, steeped in the remote familiar gloom,
What were those demons doing in that room,

Their gestures aging, where the increasing shade
Stalked the dark flame that ever wearier played
As my receding memories left me dull?
My spirit now was but a shadowy hull.
Half-lost, I felt the Lover's shame my own.
I faced the Widow; we two were alone.

I saw the head and grasped it and struck root,
And then I rose, and with a steady foot,
I left her there, retarded in a dream.
Slowly I moved, like a directed beam.
My flesh fused with the cold flesh of the head;
My blood drew from me, from the neck flowed red,
A dark pulse on the darkness. The head stirred
Weakly beneath my fingers, and I heard
A whispered laughter, and the burden grew
In life and fury as my strength withdrew.
As if I laboured up a flood of years,
I gathered heavy speed, drenched in arrears,
And limp to drowning, and I drove my flesh
Through the dark rooms adjacent to that mesh.
I was returning by the narrow hall;
Bound in my thought, jaw spread, I could not call.
And yet, with stride suspended in midair,
I fled more fast, yet more retarded there,
Swung backward by that laughter out of Hell,
Pealing at arm's length like an iron bell.

There in the darkest passage, where my feet
Fled fastest, he laughed loudest, and defeat
Was certain, for he held me in one place,
Fleeing immobile in an empty space,
I looked above me; on the stairway saw
The Widow, like a corpse. Fear drove my jaw
Wide open, and the tremor of that scream
Shattered my being like an empty dream.

THE GRAVE

Great eucalypti, black amid the flame,
Rise from below the slope, above his name.
The light is vibrant at their edges, clings,
Running in all ways through quick whisperings,
Falling in secrecy athwart each stone.
Under a little plaque he waits alone.
There is no faintest tremor in that urn.
Each flake of ash is sure in its return—
Never to alter, a pure quality,
A shadow cast against Eternity.

What has he found there? Life, it seems, is this:
To learn to shorten what has moved amiss;
To temper motion till a mean is hit,
Though the wild meaning would unbalance it;
To stand, precarious, near the utter end;
Betrayed, deserted, and alone descend,
Blackness before, and on the road above
The crowded terror that is human love;
To still the spirit till the flesh may lock
Its final cession in eternal rock.

Then let me pause in this symbolic air,
Each fiery grain immobile as despair,
Fixed at a rigid distance from the earth,
Absorbed each motion that arose from birth.
Here let me contemplate eternal peace,
Eternal station, which annuls release.
Here may I read its meaning, though the eye
Sear with the effort, ere the body die.
For what one is, one sees not; 'tis the lot
Of him at peace to contemplate it not.

ANACREONTIC

Peace! there is peace at last.
Deep in the Tuscan shade,
Swathed in the Grecian past,
Old Landor's bones are laid.

How many years have fled!
But o'er the sunken clay
Of the auguster dead
The centuries delay.

Come, write good verses, then!
That still, from age to age,
The eyes of able men
May settle on our page.

TO A YOUNG WRITER

Achilles Holt, Stanford, 1930

Here for a few short years
Strengthen affections; meet,
Later, the dull arrears
Of age, and be discreet.

The angry blood burns low.
Some friend of lesser mind
Discerns you not; but so
Your solitude's defined.

Write little; do it well.
Your knowledge will be such,
At last, as to dispel
What moves you overmuch.

TO MY INFANT DAUGHTER

I

Ah, could you now with thinking tongue
Discover what involvëd lies
In flesh and thought obscurely young,
What earth and age can worst devise!

Then I might thread my path across
Your sin and anguish; I might weigh
Minutely every gain and loss,
And time each motion of my day—

So break the impact of my wrath
To change some instant of your pain,
And clear the darkness from my path
That your decay were not in vain.

Whose hands will lay those hands to rest,
Those hands themselves, no more the same,
Will weeping lay them on the breast,
A token only and a name?

II

Alas, that I should be
So old, and you so small!
You will think naught of me
When your dire hours befall.

Take few men to your heart!
Unstable, fierce, unkind,
The ways that men impart.
True love is slow to find.

True art is slow to grow.
Like a belated friend,
It comes to let one know
Of what has had an end.

FOR MY FATHER'S GRAVE

Here lies one sweet of heart.
Stay! thou too must depart.
In silence set thy store–
These ashes speak no more.

BY THE ROAD TO THE AIR-BASE

The calloused grass lies hard
Against the cracking plain:
Life is a grayish stain;
The salt-marsh hems my yard.

Dry dikes rise hill on hill:
In sloughs of tidal slime
Shell-fish deposit lime,
Wild sea-fowl creep at will.

The highway, like a beach,
Turns whiter, shadowy, dry:
Loud, pale against the sky,
The bombing planes hold speech.

Yet fruit grows on the trees;
Here scholars pause to speak;
Through gardens bare and Greek,
I hear my neighbor's bees.

ELEGY ON A YOUNG AIREDALE BITCH LOST SOME YEARS SINCE IN THE SALT-MARSH

Low to the water's edge
You plunged; the tangled herb
Locked feet and mouth, a curb
Tough with the salty sedge.

Half dog and half a child,
Sprung from that roaming bitch,
You flung through dike and ditch,
Betrayed by what is wild.

The old dogs now are dead,
Tired with the hunt and cold,
Sunk in the earth and old.
But your bewildered head,

Led by what heron cry,
Lies by what tidal stream?—
Drenched with ancestral dream,
And cast ashore to dry.

MIDAS

Where he wandered, dream-enwound,
Brightness took the place of sound.
Shining plane and mass before:
Everywhere the sealëd door.
Children's unplacated grace
Met him with an empty face.
Mineral his limbs were grown:
Weight of being, not his own.
Ere he knew that he must die,
Ore had veinëd lip and eye:
Caught him scarcely looking back,
Startled at his golden track,
Immortalized the quickened shade
Of meaning by a moment made.

SONNET TO THE MOON

Now every leaf, though colorless, burns bright
With disembodied and celestial light,
And drops without a movement or a sound
A pillar of darkness to the shifting ground.

The lucent, thin, and alcoholic flame
Runs in the stubble with a nervous aim,
But, when the eye pursues, will point with fire
Each single stubble-tip and strain no higher.

O triple goddess! Contemplate my plight!
Opacity, my fate! Change, my delight!
The yellow tom-cat, sunk in shifting fur,
Changes and dreams, a phosphorescent blur.

Sullen I wait, but still the vision shun.
Bodiless thoughts and thoughtless bodies run.

THE ANNIVERSARY

To Achilles Holt

Where the summer stilled the vine,
We drank up a quart of wine.
Wine to parting! Man is free,
Half dissolved in memory.
Now the season is aflame,
Man has lost the way he came,
Turns confused. Momentum bends
Earth unto her fiery ends.
In the shining desert still
We must bend us to our will.
Crane is dead at sea. The year
Dwindles to a purer fear.

BEFORE DISASTER

Winter, 1932-3

Evening traffic homeward burns,
Swift and even on the turns,
Drifting weight in triple rows,
Fixed relation and repose.
This one edges out and by,
Inch by inch with steady eye.
But should error be increased,
Mass and moment are released;
Matter loosens, flooding blind,
Levels drivers to its kind.
Ranks of nations thus descend,
Watchful to a stormy end.
By a moment's calm beguiled,
I have got a wife and child.
Fool and scoundrel guide the State.
Peace is whore to Greed and Hate.
Nowhere may I turn to flee:
Action is security.
Treading change with savage heel,
We must live or die by steel.

THE PRINCE

The prince or statesman who would rise to power
Must rise through shallow trickery, and speak
The tongue of knavery, deceive the hour,
Use the corrupt, and still corrupt the weak.

And he who having power would serve the State,
Must now deceive corruption unto good,
By indirection strengthen love with hate,
Must love mankind with craft and hardihood:

Betray the witless unto wisdom, trick
Disaster to good luck, escape the gaze
Of all the pure at heart, each lunatic
Of innocence, who draws you to his daze:

And this frail balance to immortalize,
Stare publicly from death through marble eyes.

PHASELLUS ILLE

After a poem by R. P. Blackmur

The dry wood strains, the small house stands its ground:
Jointed and tough, its sides shed off the storm.
And deep within, the heavy flame is warm,
Gold weight of peace on floor and chair enwound.
Wárm mínd, wárm héart, béam, bólt, and lóck,
You hold the love you took: and now, at length,
The mind and body, in new-wedded strength,
Toughen toward age, to brace against the shock.

Hold sure the course! the small house, like a boat,
Rides firm, intact, awaits the final blow.
Beneath, the current of impartial chance,
Disaster that strikes briefly and by rote,
The hazards of insane inheritance,
Láve our smóoth húll with what we little know.

ORPHEUS

In Memory of Hart Crane

Climbing from the Lethal dead,
Past the ruined waters' bed,
In the sleep his music cast
Tree and flesh and stone were fast—
As amid Dodona's wood
Wisdom never understood.

Till the shade his music won
Shuddered, by a pause undone—
Silence would not let her stay.
He could go one only way:
By the river, strong with grief,
Gave his flesh beyond belief.

Yet the fingers on the lyre
Spread like an avenging fire.
Crying loud, the immortal tongue,
From the empty body wrung,
Broken in a bloody dream,
Sang unmeaning down the stream.

A POST-CARD TO THE SOCIAL MUSE

WHO WAS INVOKED MORE FORMALLY BY VARIOUS MARXIANS AND OTHERS IN THE PAGES OF THE NEW REPUBLIC DURING THE WINTER OF 1932-3

Madam, since you choose
To call yourself a Muse,
   I will not be too nice
      To give advice.

Passion is hard of speech,
Wisdom exact of reach;
   Poets have studied verse;
      And wit is terse.

Change or repose is wrought
By steady arm and thought:
   The fine indignant sprawl
      Confuses all.

Do not engage with those
Of small verse and less prose;
   'Twere better far to play
      At bouts-rimés.

ON THE DEATH OF SENATOR THOMAS J. WALSH

An old man more is gathered to the great.
Singly, for conscience' sake he bent his brow:
He served that mathematic thing, the State,
And with the great will be forgotten now.
The State is voiceless: only, we may write
Singly our thanks for service past, and praise
The man whose purpose and remorseless sight
Pursued corruption for its evil ways.

How sleep the great, the gentle, and the wise!
Agëd and calm, they couch the wrinkled head.
Done with the wisdom that mankind devise,
Humbly they render back the volume read—
Dwellers amid a peace that few surmise,
Masters of quiet among all the dead.

DEDICATION FOR A BOOK OF CRITICISM

To W. D. Briggs

He who learns may feed on lies:
He who understands is wise.
He who understands the great
Joins them in their own estate:
Grasping what they had to give,
Adds his strength that they may live.

Strong the scholar is to scan
What is permanent in man;
To detect his form and kind
And preserve the human mind;
By the type himself to guide,
Universal wisdom bide.

Heir of Linacre and More,
Guardian of Erasmus' store,
Careful knower of the best,
Bacon's scholar, Jonson's guest,
It was in your speaking lip
That I honored scholarship.

In the motions of your thought
I a plan and model sought;
My deficiencies but gauge
My own talents and the age;
What is good from you I took:
Then, in justice, take my book.

A LEAVE-TAKING

I, who never kissed your head,
Lay these ashes in their bed;
That which I could do have done.
Now farewell, my newborn son.

ON TEACHING THE YOUNG

The young are quick of speech.
Grown middle-aged, I teach
Corrosion and distrust,
Exacting what I must.

A poem is what stands
When imperceptive hands,
Feeling, have gone astray.
It is what one should say.

Few minds will come to this.
The poet's only bliss
Is in cold certitude—
Laurel, archaic, rude.

CHIRON

I, who taught Achilles, saw
Leap beyond me by its law,
By intrinsic law destroyed,
Genius in itself alloyed.

Dying scholar, dim with fact,
By the stallion body racked,
Studying my long defeat,
I have mastered Jove's deceit.

Now my head is bald and dried,
Past division simplified:
On the edge of naught I wait,
Magnitude inviolate.

HERACLES

For Don Stanford

Eurystheus, trembling, called me to the throne,
Alcmena's son, heavy with thews and still.
He drove me on my fatal road alone:
I went, subservient to Hera's will.

For, when I had resisted, she had struck
Out of the sky and spun my wit: I slew
My children, quicker than a stroke of luck,
With motion lighter than my sinews knew.

Compelled down ways obscure with analogue
To force the Symbols of the Zodiac—
Bright Lion, Boundless Hydra, Fiery Dog—
I spread them on my arms as on a rack:

Spread them and broke them in the groaning wood,
And yet the Centaur stung me from afar,
His blood envenomed with the Hydra's blood:
Thence was I outcast from the earthy war.

Nessus the Centaur, with his wineskin full,
His branch and thyrsus, and his fleshy grip—
Her whom he could not force he yet could gull.
And she drank poison from his bearded lip.

Older than man, evil with age, is life:
Injustice, direst perfidy, my bane
Drove me to win my lover and my wife;
By love and justice I at last was slain.

The numbered Beings of the wheeling track
I carried singly to the empty throne,
And yet, when I had come exhausted back,
Was forced to wait without the gate alone.

Commanded thus to pause before the gate,
I felt from my hot breast the tremors pass,

White flame dissecting the corrupted State,
Eurystheus vibrant in his den of brass:

Vibrant with horror, though a jewelled king,
Lest, the heat mounting, madness turn my brain
For one dry moment, and the palace ring
With crystal terror ere I turn again.

This stayed me, too: my life was not my own,
But I my life's; a god I was, not man.
Grown Absolute, I slew my flesh and bone;
Timeless, I knew the Zodiac my span.

This was my grief, that out of grief I grew—
Translated as I was from earth at last,
From the sad pain that Deïanira knew.
Transmuted slowly in a fiery blast,

Perfect, and moving perfectly, I raid
Eternal silence to eternal ends:
And Deïanira, an imperfect shade,
Retreats in silence as my arc descends.

ALCMENA

Now praise Alcmena for unchanging pride!
She sent her lover, when her brothers died,
To carry bloody death, where death was just;
The vengeance done, she yielded to his lust.
Zeus in the Theban halls her love besought:
To Zeus the greatest of his sons she brought:
The scion whom the god desired her for,
Alcides, Hero of Symbolic War.
She long outlived Alcides; when his son
Destroyed Eurystheus, and the feud was done,
She gouged the tyrant's eyes and cursed the head.
Then dense with age, she laid her on her bed.
But Zeus remembered the unbending dame,
Her giant maidenhood, the tireless frame,
That long had honored and had served him well,
And made her Rhadamanthus' queen in Hell.

THESEUS: A TRILOGY

For Henry Ramsey

I. THE WRATH OF ARTEMIS

On the wet sand the queen emerged from forest,
Tall as a man, half naked, and at ease,
Leaned on her bow and eyed them. This, the priestess,
Who, with her savages, had harried Greece
From south to east, and now fought down from Thrace,
Her arrows cold as moonlight, and her flesh
Bright as her arrows, and her hatred still.
Heracles eyed the ground, and Theseus watched her.
Remote and thin as a bird-call over ice
From deep in the forest came the cry of her warriors,
Defiance from Artemis, the evasive daemon:
Hippolyta smiled, but Heracles moved softly
And seized her suddenly, bore her to the ship,
Bound her and left her vibrating like a deer,
Astounded beyond terror. And her women
Fell as they came, like water to dry earth,
An inundation of the living moon.

From out the close hold of the nervous galley
She heard the shouting muffled in soft blood;
She heard it thinning quietly away.
And anger seized her; mind exceeded body,
Invoked divinity and rose to godhead:
She prayed the goddess to avenge the dead.
Then, in the doorway, blackened with maiden death,
Appeared the Attic conqueror in fulfillment.
Theseus, inexorable with love and war,
And ignorant with youth, begot upon her
A son, created in her shuddering fury,
To be born in Attica, the naked land.

In Attica, the naked land, she strode,
Brooding upon the secrets of the goddess,
Upon the wet bark of the Scythian forest,
The wet turf under bare foot, and the night
Blue with insistence of the staring eye.

The son, conceived in hatred, grew implacably,
Beyond her slow death, which he saw in passing,
Insolent, slender, effeminate, and chill,
His muscles made for running down the stag,
Dodging the boar, which Theseus would have broken,
Keeping step with the moon's shadows, changing
From thought to thought with an unchanging face.
He, judging Theseus from his narrow wisdom,
Yet judged him, and exiled him from his quiet,
The wrath of Artemis grown part of Theseus,
A man of moonlight and intensive calm.

II. THESEUS AND ARIADNE

After the mossy night and the wet stone,
The grappling with the wet hair of the beast,
After the slow and careful fingering
Of the pale linen on the cold return,
Theseus emerged. Ariadne awaited him,
Her face half hidden with black hair and shame.

And Theseus spoke:
The Minotaur is dead.
Pasiphaë the white will sin no more:
The daughter of the moon, who bore this ghast
And dripping horror has been long at rest.
The sin of your blood I have extinguished; yet
Think not you will go quit. Your body is mine,
By all these tokens; and the taint of hell
Has eaten through my skin. Minos contrived
The trembling blackness of that hall of vision;
The prisoned fiend, your brother, beat me down,
I drew him after, and his blood burned through me,
Stinging more wildly than your body.
She:
My mother's sin has poisoned you, and I
Was poisoned long ago. We share this crime,
And I am yours, I know not to what end.
Minos' vengeance is buried in our two bodies.
You had me from Minos, should you prevail,

And Minos is the will of Zeus, withdraws not.
I am motionless in the scales of Justice.
We go now to your ship; the carven wood
Will glide in quiet from the rocks of Crete,
That bloodstained island of the gods, and we
Shall set our feet in peace on lesser isles.

So Theseus took her by the hand, boarded
The limber galley, and the foam distended
Coldly above the crash on rock. The boat,
Quick on the heavy tumult, scoured the inlets
And found that island where he slew her, yet
Escaped not, took her sister, her for whom
Poseidon betrayed him, when he slew his son.

III. THE OLD AGE OF THESEUS

He gathered Phaedra, hard with childhood, small,
Shivering in arm and breast, into his arms.
He knew his age at last. Sin with this child
Was sin in solitude. Arms that had bound
The Heraclean bull, Phaea the sow,
That had fought side by side with Heracles
And beat their black way from the ice of Lethe,
Were hard with realized identity,
Beyond her comprehension, and he lay
Whole in the salty toughness of his age.

When he set foot in Attica, he found
Aegeus at rest, and he assumed the State.
Here were abstractions fitter for his years:
The calculation of corruption, thus
To balance evil against evil surely
And establish immitigable good.

He ruled
Hard in his certitude through Phaedra's death,
The betrayal of his son, that eccentricity
Of furious children. And he gathered up
The knowledge of his youth: the steady shame
Of tall Hippolyta; the calm of Aethra;

The quiet evil of the grave Medea;
The image of Pirithoüs in Hell,
Caught in the moving flesh among the shades—
Passion immovable!—the Orphic music
That swelled the measure of the Argo's oars
To a golden stride coëval with the Sun—
Gathered them slowly up and fed upon them,
Distilled from them the honey of calm wisdom—
The face of Ariadne dead, himself
Suddenly translated to another time.

Alone, he and the State. The State, established,
Exiled him into Scyros. Lycomedes,
The strange face of a king, was all that stood
Between him and himself. And Lycomedes,
The treacherous host, betrayed him to the State,
Which had betrayed him, to which he had been betrayed
By every movement of his flesh and spirit;
So cast him from the rock to solitude,
To the cold perfection of unending peace.

SOCRATES

For Clayton Stafford

We come now to the hemlock: this, the test
Of my daimonic promptings, of my long
Uncertain labor to discern the best,
To formulate forever what is wrong.

What is the city? What historic crux
Have we approached? Could but my skill endure,
The mind of Athens might surpass the flux,
When tongue and stone subside, her thought be sure.

If of my talking there should come a soul
Of tougher thought in richer phrase empearled,
Then were I sire and grandsire, scroll by scroll,
The vast foundation of a Western World.

While arguing amid the colonnades,
Tired in the noon-day by the badly taught,
Or resting, dubious, in the laurel shades,
I have impinged upon a firmer thought;

Have raised the Timeless up against the times;
The times, in turn, with this insensate cup,
Judge definition the most fierce of crimes;
The Timeless bids me drink the judgment up.

Thus are the times transmuted: understood,
A Timeless Form, comprising my estate.
Though what escapes them is my proper good,
Yet still would I be, so must they be, great.

Consistency gives quiet to the end.
My enemy is but a type of man,
And him whom I have changed, I call my friend.
The mind is formed. Dissuade it, he who can.

TO EDWIN V. McKENZIE

On his defense of David Lamson

The concept lives, but few men fill the frame;
Greatness is difficult: the certain aim,
The powerful body, and the nervous skill,
The acquiring mind, and the untiring will,
The just man's fury and uplifted arm,
And the strong heart, to keep the weak from harm.
This is the great man of tradition, one
To point out justice when the wrong is done;
To outwit rogue and craven; represent
Mankind in the eternal sacrament—
Odysseus, with the giant weapon bent.

When those who guard tradition in the schools
Proved to be weaklings and half-learnëd fools,
You took the burden, saved the intellect.
Combating treason, mastering each defect,
You fought your battle, inch by inch of ground.
When Justice had become an angry sound,
When Judgment dwindled to an angry man,
You named the limits of the civil span:
I saw you, mantled in tradition, tower;
You filled the courtroom with historic power;
Yourself the concept in the final hour.

TO A WOMAN ON HER DEFENSE OF HER BROTHER UNJUSTLY CONVICTED OF MURDER

Written after an initial study of the evidence

The villainy of pride in scholarship,
The villainy of cold impartial hate,
The brutal quiet of the lying lip,
The brutal power, judicial and sedate,

The calculation of the shifting friend,
The changing eye, the closed and narrowing scene,
The steady vision of the awful end,
Outrage and anarchy in formal mien;

These for an evil year now you have fought,
Which for three weeks, through nervous nights awake,
I learned could break me, for the Devil wrought.
May God support you, for your brother's sake!

There is a special Hell for each of these:
The brute, succumbing where his judgments err,
Compels the cringing fool to perjuries;
The friend begs comfort of the perjurer;

The scholar, now discovering his allies,
And turning to himself to stay his doom,
Finds but his pride amid a nest of lies,
A dire obsession in an empty room.

And what of him whom men at last disown!
Whom circumstance, guided by evil will,
Struck when his mind had broken! Locked in stone,
He waits the summons of the State to kill.

Ah, should you lose at last, yet you and he,
Each in the certitude the other gave,
Strong in your love, and by your love made free,
Would bear some goodness to the utter grave!

Yet may you two, bound in a stronger whole,
Firm in disaster, amid evil true,
Give us some knowledge of the human soul
And bend our spirits to the human due!

TO DAVID LAMSON

Awaiting retrial, in the jail at San José

If I ever pleased the Muse,
May she not one boon refuse;
May I ages hence rehearse
Darkest evil in my verse;
May I state my grief and shame
At the scholar's empty name:
How great scholars failed to see
Virtue in extremity;
How the special intellect
Fortified them in neglect,
Left their feelings, brutal, wild,
By inconsequence beguiled;
Wisdom brought to final rest,
Learning's very name a jest,
And the wise, like village fools,
County politicians' tools;
How I found a quiet friend,
Working at the evening's end,
Far beyond the tongues that rail,
Hidden in the county jail,
Who, unchanged amid disease,
Wrote with power and spoke with ease,
Who, though human thought decayed,
Yet the dissolution stayed,
Gracious in that evil shade.

JOHN DAY, FRONTIERSMAN

Among the first and farthest! Elk and deer
Fell as your rifle rang in rocky caves;
There your lean shadow swept the still frontier,
Your eyes regarded the Columbia's waves.

Amid the stony winter, gray with care,
Hunted by savages from sleep to sleep
—Those patriots of darkness and despair!—
You climbed in solitude what rigid steep!

Broken at last by very force of frame,
By wintry hunger like a warrior's brand,
You died a madman. And now bears your name
A gentle river in a fertile land.

The eminence is gone that met your eye;
The winding savage, too, has sunk away.
Now, like a summer myth, the meadows lie,
Deep in the calm of silvan slow decay.

JOHN SUTTER

I was the patriarch of the shining land,
Of the blond summer and metallic grain;
Men vanished at the motion of my hand,
And when I beckoned they would come again.

The earth grew dense with grain at my desire;
The shade was deepened at the springs and streams;
Moving in dust that clung like pillared fire,
The gathering herds grew heavy in my dreams.

Across the mountains, naked from the heights,
Down to the valley broken settlers came,
And in my houses feasted through the nights,
Rebuilt their sinews and assumed a name.

In my clear rivers my own men discerned
The motive for the ruin and the crime—
Gold heavier than earth, a wealth unearned,
Loot, for two decades, from the heart of Time.

Metal, intrinsic value, deep and dense,
Preanimate, inimitable, still,
Real, but an evil with no human sense,
Dispersed the mind to concentrate the will.

Grained by alchemic change, the human kind
Turned from themselves to rivers and to rocks;
With dynamite broke metal unrefined;
Measured their moods by geologic shocks.

With knives they dug the metal out of stone;
Turned rivers back, for gold through ages piled,
Drove knives to hearts, and faced the gold alone;
Valley and river ruined and reviled;

Reviled and ruined me, my servant slew,
Strangled him from the figtree by my door.
When they had done what fury bade them do,
I was a cursing beggar, stripped and sore.

What end impersonal, what breathless age,
Incontinent of quiet and of years,
What calm catastrophe will yet assuage
This final drouth of penitential tears?

THE CALIFORNIA OAKS

Spreading and low, unwatered, concentrate
Of years of growth that thickens, not expands,
With leaves like mica and with roots that grate
Upon the deep foundations of these lands,
In your brown shadow, on your heavy loam
—Leaves shrinking to the whisper of decay—
What feet have come to roam,
what eyes to stay?
Your motion has o'ertaken what calm hands?

Quick as a sunbeam, when a bird divides
The lesser branches, on impassive ground,
Hwui-Shan, the ancient, for a moment glides,
Demure with wisdom, and without a sound;
Brown feet that come to meet him, quick and shy,
Move in the flesh, then, browner, dry to bone;
The brook-like shadows lie
where sun had shone;
Ceaseless, the dead leaves gather, mound on mound.

And where they gather, darkening the glade,
In hose and doublet, and with knotty beard,
Armed with the musket and the pirate's blade,
Stern as the silence by the savage feared,
Drake and his seamen pause to view the hills,
Measure the future with a steady gaze.
But when they go naught fills
the patient days;
The bay lies empty where the vessels cleared.

The Spaniard, learning caution from the trees,
Building his dwelling from the native clay,
Took native concubines: the blood of these
Calming his blood, he made a longer stay.
Longer, but yet recessive, for the change
Came on his sons and their sons to the end;

For peace may yet derange
and earth may bend
The ambitious mind to an archaic way.

Then the invasion! and the soil was turned,
The hidden waters drained, the valleys dried;
And whether fire or purer sunlight burned,
No matter! one by one the old oaks died.
Died or are dying! The archaic race—
Black oak, live oak, and valley oak—ere long
Must crumble on the place
which they made strong
And in the calm they guarded now abide.

ON REREADING A PASSAGE FROM JOHN MUIR

Seeking in vain to find the heroic brow,
The subject fitting for a native ode,
I turn from thinking, for there haunts me now
A wrinkled figure on a dusty road:
Climbing from road to path, from path to rock,
From rock to live oak, thence to mountain bay,
Through unmoved twilight, where the rifle's shock
Was half absorbed by leaves and drawn away,
Through mountain lilac, where the brown deer lay.

This was my childhood's revery: to be
Not one who seeks in nature his release
But one forever by the dripping tree,
Paradisaïc in his pristine peace.
I might have been this man: a knowing eye
Moving on leaf and bark, a quiet gauge
Of growing timber and of climbing fly,
A quiet hand to fix them on the page—
A gentle figure from a simpler age.

THE MANZANITA

Under the forest, where the day is dark
And air is motionless throughout the day,
Rooted in leaf-mould and in rotting bark,
This old arbutus gathers strength to stay.

Tall as a man, and taller, but more old,
This is no shrub of some few years, but hard
Its smooth unbending trunk, oh, hard and cold!
Of earth and age the stony proof and guard!

The skin is rose: yet infinitely thin,
It is a color only. What one tells
Of ancient wood and softly glinting skin
Is less than are the tiny waxen bells.

This life is not our life; nor for our wit
The sweetness of these shades; these are alone.
There is no wisdom here; seek not for it!
This is the shadow of the vast madrone.

SIR GAWAINE AND THE GREEN KNIGHT

Reptilian green the wrinkled throat,
Green as a bough of yew the beard;
He bent his head, and so I smote;
Then for a thought my vision cleared.

The head dropped clean; he rose and walked;
He fixed his fingers in the hair;
The head was unabashed and talked;
I understood what I must dare.

His flesh, cut down, arose and grew.
He bade me wait the season's round,
And then, when he had strength anew,
To meet him on his native ground.

The year declined; and in his keep
I passed in joy a thriving yule;
And whether waking or in sleep,
I lived in riot like a fool.

He beat the woods to bring me meat.
His lady, like a forest vine,
Grew in my arms; the growth was sweet;
And yet what thoughtless force was mine!

By practice and conviction formed,
With ancient stubbornness ingrained,
Although her body clung and swarmed,
My own identity remained.

Her beauty, lithe, unholy, pure,
Took shapes that I had never known;
And had I once been insecure,
Had grafted laurel in my bone.

And then, since I had kept the trust,
Had loved the lady, yet was true,
The knight withheld his giant thrust
And let me go with what I knew.

I left the green bark and the shade,
Where growth was rapid, thick, and still;
I found a road that men had made
And rested on a drying hill.

AN OCTOBER NOCTURNE

October 31st, 1936

The night was faint and sheer;
Immobile, road and dune.
Then, for a moment, clear,
A plane moved past the moon.

O spirit cool and frail,
Hung in the lunar fire!
Spun wire and brittle veil!
And trembling slowly higher!

Pure in each proven line!
The balance and the aim,
Half empty, half divine!
I saw how true you came.

Dissevered from your cause,
Your function was your goal.
Oblivious of my laws,
You made your calm patrol.

A SPRING SERPENT

The little snake now grieves
With whispering pause, and slow,
Uncertain where to go
Among the glassy leaves,
Pale angel that deceives.

With tongue too finely drawn,
Too pure, too tentative,
He needs but move to live,
Yet where he was is gone;
He loves the quiet lawn.

Kin to the petal, cool,
Translucent, veinëd, firm,
The fundamental worm,
The undefinëd fool,
Dips to the icy pool.

MUCH IN LITTLE

Amid the iris and the rose,
The honeysuckle and the bay,
The wild earth for a moment goes
In dust or weed another way.

Small though its corner be, the weed
Will yet intrude its creeping beard;
The harsh blade and the hairy seed
Recall the brutal earth we feared.

And if no water touch the dust
In some far corner, and one dare
To breathe upon it, one may trust
The spectre on the summer air:

The risen dust alive with fire,
The fire made visible, a blur
Interrate, the pervasive ire
Of foxtail and of hoarhound burr.

THE CREMATION

E. H. L.: 1866-1938

In Egypt, these five thousand years,
Men char with time, yet undispersed.
But we, whose mortal vision clears,
In one compact and final crash
In which a lifetime is reversed,
Sever the body from its ash.

The ash is but a little dust,
The body is eternal light.
And where is that which made you just?
Which gathered light about the bone
And moved the tongue, in earth's despite?
The powdered lime sinks back alone.

Thus you have left a fainter trace
Of what the spirit bore for hire
—No bony outline of a face!—
Than ages of the drying dead.
Once and for all you went through fire:
There is no footprint where you tread.

AN ELEGY

For the U.S.N. Dirigible, Macon

The noon is beautiful: the perfect wheel
Now glides on perfect surface with a sound
Earth has not heard before; the polished ground
Trembles and whispers under rushing steel.

The polished ground, and prehistoric air!
Metal now plummets upward and there sways,
A loosened pendulum for summer days,
Fixing the eyeball in a limpid stare.

There was one symbol in especial, one
Great form of thoughtless beauty that arose
Above the mountains, to foretell the close
Of this deception, at meridian.

Steel-gray the shadow, than a storm more vast!
Its crowding engines, rapid, disciplined,
Shook the great valley like a rising wind.
This image, now, is conjured from the past.

Wind in the wind! O form more light than cloud!
Storm amid storms! And by the storms dispersed!
The brain-drawn metal rose until accursed
By its extension and the sky was loud!

Who will believe this thing in time to come?
I was a witness. I beheld the age
That seized upon a planet's heritage
Of steel and oil, the mind's viaticum:

Crowded the world with strong ingenious things,
Used the provision it could not replace,
To leave but Cretan myths, a sandy trace
Through the last stone age, for the pastoral kings.

TIME AND THE GARDEN

The spring has darkened with activity.
The future gathers in vine, bush, and tree:
Persimmon, walnut, loquat, fig, and grape,
Degrees and kinds of color, taste, and shape.
These will advance in their due series, space
The season like a tranquil dwelling-place.
And yet excitement swells me, vein by vein:
I long to crowd the little garden, gain
Its sweetness in my hand and crush it small
And taste it in a moment, time and all!
These trees, whose slow growth measures off my years,
I would expand to greatness. No one hears,
And I am still retarded in duress!
And this is like that other restlessness
To seize the greatness not yet fairly earned,
One which the tougher poets have discerned—
Gascoigne, Ben Jonson, Greville, Raleigh, Donne,
Poets who wrote great poems, one by one,
And spaced by many years, each line an act
Through which few labor, which no men retract.
This passion is the scholar's heritage,
The imposition of a busy age,
The passion to condense from book to book
Unbroken wisdom in a single look,
Though we know well that when this fix the head,
The mind's immortal, but the man is dead.

TO A PORTRAIT OF MELVILLE IN MY LIBRARY

O face reserved, unmoved by praise or scorn!
O dreadful heart that won Socratic peace!
What was the purchase-price of thy release?
What life was buried, ere thou rose reborn?
Rest here in quiet, now. Our strength is shorn.
Honor my books! Preserve this room from wrack!
Plato and Aristotle at thy back,
Above thy head this ancient powder-horn.

The lids droop coldly, and the face is still:
Wisdom and wilderness are here at poise,
Ocean and forest are the mind's device,
But still I feel the presence of thy will:
The midnight trembles when I hear thy voice,
The noon's immobile when I meet thine eyes.

A PRAYER FOR MY SON

'Tangled with earth all ways we move.'
—Janet Lewis

Eternal Spirit, you
Whose will maintains the world,
Who thought and made it true;
The honey-suckle curled
Through the arbutus limb,
The leaves that move in air,
Are half akin to him
Whose conscious moving stare
Is drawn, yet stirs by will;
Whose little fingers bend,
Unbend, and then are still,
While the mind seeks an end.
At moments, like a vine,
He clambers through small boughs;
Then poised and half divine,
He waits with lifted brows.
To steep the mind in sense,
Yet never lose the aim,
Will make the world grow dense,
Yet by this way we came.
Earth and mind are not one,
But they are so entwined,
That this, my little son,
May yet one day go blind.
Eternal Spirit, you
Who guided Socrates,
Pity this small and new
Bright soul on hands and knees.

IN PRAISE OF CALIFORNIA WINES

Amid these clear and windy hills
Heat gathers quickly and is gone;
Dust rises, moves, and briefly stills;
Our thought can scarcely pause thereon.

With pale bright leaf and shadowy stem,
Pellucid amid nervous dust,
By pre-Socratic stratagem,
Yet sagging with its weight of must,

The vineyard spreads beside the road
In repetition, point and line.
I sing, in this dry bright abode,
The praises of the native wine.

It yields the pleasure of the eye,
It charms the skin, it warms the heart;
When nights are cold and thoughts crowd high,
Then 'tis the solvent for our art.

When worn for sleep the head is dull,
When art has failed us, far behind,
Its sweet corruption fills the skull
Till we are happy to be blind.

So may I yet, as poets use,
My time being spent, and more to pay,
In this quick warmth the will diffuse,
In sunlight vanish quite away.

A SUMMER COMMENTARY

When I was young, with sharper sense,
The farthest insect cry I heard
Could stay me; through the trees, intense,
I watched the hunter and the bird.

Where is the meaning that I found?
Or was it but a state of mind,
Some old penumbra of the ground,
In which to be but not to find?

Now summer grasses, brown with heat,
Have crowded sweetness through the air;
The very roadside dust is sweet;
Even the unshadowed earth is fair.

The soft voice of the nesting dove,
And the dove in soft erratic flight
Like a rapid hand within a glove,
Caress the silence and the light.

Amid the rubble, the fallen fruit,
Fermenting in its rich decay,
Smears brandy on the trampling boot
And sends it sweeter on its way.

ON THE PORTRAIT OF A SCHOLAR OF THE ITALIAN RENAISSANCE

The color, quick in fluid oil,
Affirms the flesh and lambent hair;
And darkness, in its fine recoil,
Confesses that the mind is there.

With heavy lip, with massive curls,
With wisdom weighted, strong and dense,
The flesh is luminous as pearls;
The eyes ingenuous but intense.

The face is noble; but the name
Is one that we shall scarcely hold.
This is a vision in a frame,
Defined and matted down with gold.

Our names, with his, are but the lees
Residual from this clear intent;
Our finely grained identities
Are but this golden sediment.

A DEDICATION IN POSTSCRIPT

for my poems of 1940
Written to Agnes Lee shortly before her death

Because you labored still for Gautier's strength
In days when art was lost in breadth and length;
Because your friendship was a valued gift;
I send these poems—now, my only shift.
In the last years of your declining age,
I face again your cold immortal page:
The statue, pure amid the rotting leaves,
And her, forsaken, whom Truth undeceives.
Truth is the subject, and the hand is sure.
The hand once lay in mine: this will endure
Till all the casual errors fall away.
And art endures, or so the masters say.

A WINTER EVENING

near Alviso, California

The earth for miles is massed with wet:
Small tree and bush and hedge of briar
Have sunk from shape with help nor let
As rank confusion gathers higher.

Each little house beside the road,
In weedy field, with rotting fence,
Groans and subsides, a broken load
Dropped there by thwarted diligence.

And by a swollen ditch, a dog,
Mud-soaked and happy, in a daze
Works into rain as dark as fog,
And moves down coldly solvent ways.

SUMMER NOON: 1941

With visionary care
The mind imagines Hell,
Draws fine the sound of flame
Till one can scarcely tell
The nature, or the name,
Or what the thing is for:
   Past summer bough and cry,
The sky, distended, bare,
Now whispers like a shell
Of the increase of war.
   Thus will man reach an end:
In fear of his own will,
Yet moved where it may tend,
With mind and word grown still.
   The fieldmouse and the hare,
The small snake of the garden,
Whose little muscles harden,
Whose eyes now quickened stare,
Though driven by the sound
—Too small and free to pardon!—
Will repossess this ground.

A TESTAMENT

To one now a child

We will and move: the gain
Is purchased with our pain;
  The very strength we choose
    With what we lose.

God is revealed in this:
That some go not amiss,
  But through hard labor teach
    What we may reach.

These gave us life through death:
Jesus of Nazareth,
  Archaic Socrates,
    And such as these.

O small and fair of face!
In this appalling place,
  The conscious soul must give
    Its life to live.

TO A MILITARY RIFLE

1942

The times come round again;
The private life is small;
And individual men
Are counted not at all.
Now life is general,
And the bewildered Muse,
Thinking what she has done,
Confronts the daily news.

Blunt emblem, you have won:
With carven stock unbroke,
With core of steel, with crash
Of mass, and fading smoke;
Your fire leaves little ash;
Your balance on the arm
Points whither you intend;
Your bolt is smooth with charm.
When other concepts end,
This concept, hard and pure,
Shapes every mind therefor.
The time is yours, be sure,
Old Hammerheel of War.

I cannot write your praise
When young men go to die;
Nor yet regret the ways
That ended with this hour.
The hour has come. And I,
Who alter nothing, pray
That men, surviving you,
May learn to do and say
The difficult and true,
True shape of death and power.

FOR THE OPENING OF THE WILLIAM DINSMORE BRIGGS ROOM*

Stanford University, May 7, 1942

Because our Being grows in mind,
And evil in imperfect thought,
And passion running undefined
May ruin what the masters taught;

Within the edge of war we meet
To dedicate this room to one
Who made his wisdom more complete
Than any save the great have done.

That in this room, men yet may reach,
By labor and wit's sullen shock,
The final certitude of speech
Which Hell itself cannot unlock.

MOONLIGHT ALERT

Los Altos, California, June 1943

The sirens, rising, woke me; and the night
Lay cold and windless; and the moon was bright,
Moonlight from sky to earth, untaught, unclaimed,
An icy nightmare of the brute unnamed.
This was hallucination. Scarlet flower
And yellow fruit hung colorless. That hour
No scent lay on the air. The siren scream
Took on the fixity of shallow dream.
In the dread sweetness I could see the fall,
Like petals sifting from a quiet wall,
Of yellow soldiers through indifferent air,
Falling to die in solitude. With care
I held this vision, thinking of young men
Whom I had known and should not see again,
Fixed in reality, as I in thought.
And I stood waiting, and encountered naught.

*A reading room for graduate students in English, established as a memorial to the late head of the Stanford English department.

DEFENSE OF EMPIRE

The nervous light above my door
Towers high with blossoms; all their scent
Is shaken with the climbing roar
Of planes which thread the firmament.

Young men, preoccupied, alone,
Learn to control the earth and air;
Yet what is mine should be their own
And interpenetrate their care:

The perils of immortal mind,
The core of empire in a word,
The worth of states grown hard to find
Because true meaning is unheard;

The deviation from the strength
Which forms our motion, and the phrase
Which cheapens thought and yet at length
Would simulate more honest ways;

This fine deceit, this perfect rift,
Dissociating thought from sense,
I traced in quiet; and the shrift
Of wrath was all my recompense.

NIGHT OF BATTLE

Europe: 1944
as regarded from a great distance

Impersonal the aim
Where giant movements tend;
Each man appears the same;
Friend vanishes from friend.

In the long path of lead
That changes place like light
No shape of hand or head
Means anything tonight.

Only the common will
For which explosion spoke;
And stiff on field and hill
The dark blood of the folk.

AN ODE ON THE DESPOILERS OF LEARNING IN AN AMERICAN UNIVERSITY: 1947

This was our heritage:
In Learning's monument
To study, and teach the young,
Until our days were spent;
To reëmbody mind
In age succeeding age,
That some few men might see,
Though, mostly, men were blind;
To hold what men had wrung
From struggle to atone
For man's stupidity,
In labor and alone.

But now the insensate, calm
Performers of the hour,
Cold, with cold eye and palm,
Desiring trivial power,
And terror-struck within
At their own emptiness,
Move in. As they move in,
Slow and invidious,
They pause and calculate,
Then, as such beings use,
With long-perfected hate,
Strike the immortal Muse.

What art of prose or verse
Should bring their like to book?
What consecrated curse
And pious rhetoric?
Not one: we need but look.
For these have come too far:
They stand here, coarse and lined,
And permanent as stone,
In the final light of mind.
The body politic
Of Learning is its own
Inscrutable old Bar.

TO HERMAN MELVILLE IN 1951

Saint Herman, grant me this: that I may be
Saved from the worms who have infested thee.

TO THE HOLY SPIRIT

from a deserted graveyard
in the Salinas Valley

Immeasurable haze:
The desert valley spreads
Up golden river-beds
As if in other days.
Trees rise and thin away,
And past the trees, the hills,
Pure line and shade of dust,
Bear witness to our wills:
We see them, for we must;
Calm in deceit, they stay.

High noon returns the mind
Upon its local fact:
Dry grass and sand; we find
No vision to distract.
Low in the summer heat,
Naming old graves, are stones
Pushed here and there, the seat
Of nothing, and the bones
Beneath are similar:
Relics of lonely men,
Brutal and aimless, then,
As now, irregular.

These are thy fallen sons,
Thou whom I try to reach.
Thou whom the quick eye shuns,
Thou dost elude my speech.
Yet when I go from sense
And trace thee down in thought,

I meet thee, then, intense,
And know thee as I ought.
But thou art mind alone,
And I, alas, am bound
Pure mind to flesh and bone,
And flesh and bone to ground.

These had no thought: at most
Dark faith and blinding earth.
Where is the trammeled ghost?
Was there another birth?
Only one certainty
Beside thine unfleshed eye,
Beside the spectral tree,
Can I discern: these die.
All of this stir of age,
Though it elude my sense
Into what heritage
I know not, seems to fall,
Quiet beyond recall,
Into irrelevance.

A FRAGMENT

I cannot find my way to Nazareth.
I have had enough of this. Thy will is death,
And this unholy quiet is thy peace.
Thy will be done; and let discussion cease.

A SONG IN PASSING

Where am I now? And what
Am I to say portends?
Death is but death, and not
The most obtuse of ends.

No matter how one leans
One yet fears not to know.
God knows what all this means!
The mortal mind is slow.

Eternity is here.
There is no other place.
The only thing I fear
Is the Almighty Face.

TO THE MOON

Goddess of poetry,
Maiden of icy stone
With no anatomy,
Between us two alone
Your light falls thin and sure
On all that I propound.

Your service I have found
To be no sinecure;
For I must still inure
My words to what I find,
Though it should leave me blind
Ere I discover how.

What brings me here? Old age.
Here is the written page.
What is your pleasure now?

AT THE SAN FRANCISCO AIRPORT

To my daughter, 1954

This is the terminal: the light
Gives perfect vision, false and hard;
The metal glitters, deep and bright.
Great planes are waiting in the yard–
They are already in the night.

And you are here beside me, small,
Contained and fragile, and intent
On things that I but half recall–
Yet going whither you are bent.
I am the past, and that is all.

But you and I in part are one:
The frightened brain, the nervous will,
The knowledge of what must be done,
The passion to acquire the skill
To face that which you dare not shun.

The rain of matter upon sense
Destroys me momently. The score:
There comes what will come. The expense
Is what one thought, and something more–
One's being and intelligence.

This is the terminal, the break.
Beyond this point, on lines of air,
You take the way that you must take;
And I remain in light and stare–
In light, and nothing else, awake.

TWO OLD-FASHIONED SONGS

I. DANSE MACABRE

Who was who and where were they
Scholars all and bound to go
Iambs without heel or toe
Something one would never say
Moving in a certain way

Students with an empty book
Poets neither here nor there
Critics without face or hair
Something had them on the hook
Here was neither king nor rook

This is something some one said
I was wrong and he was right
Indirection in the night
Every second move was dead
Though I came I went instead

II. A DREAM VISION

What was all the talk about?
This was something to decide.
It was not that I had died.
Though my plans were new, no doubt,
There was nothing to deride.

I had grown away from youth,
Shedding error where I could;
I was now essential wood,
Concentrating into truth;
What I did was small but good.

Orchard tree beside the road,
Bare to core, but living still!
Moving little was my skill.
I could hear the farting toad
Shifting to observe the kill,

Spotted sparrow, spawn of dung,
Mumbling on a horse's turd,
Bullfinch, wren, or mockingbird
Screaming with a pointed tongue
Objurgation without word.

NOTES

For the reader who may not be familiar with some of the reference books which have beguiled my own leisure, I offer the following clarifications:

'The Invaders' (p. 117). The Invaders are the modern physical scientists, of whom I would not write in quite the same terms today.

'The Castle of Thorns' (p. 118). In medieval romance, which is for the most part a refurbishing of ancient folklore, the Robber Knight commonly represents Death. In taking his victim to his castle, which is normally surrounded by a wood of thorn, he must in some way cross or dive under water, which is the most ancient symbol of the barrier between the two worlds.

'Heracles' (pp. 147-8). Heracles is treated as a Sun-god, the particular statement used being that of Anthon's *Classical Dictionary*. Allegorically he is the artist in hand-to-hand or semi-intuitive combat with experience.

'The California Oaks' (pp. 160-1). There is a brief account of Hwui-Shan on pages 24-5 of *A History of California: the Spanish Period*, by Charles Edward Chapman. Hwui-Shan was a Chinese Buddhist priest, who may have come to California in 499 A.D. According to Chapman, the story is found in Volume 231 of the great Chinese Encyclopedia and in other works, and has long been known to Chinese scholars. Chapman believes that there were other Chinese voyages to the west coast of North America at very early dates.

III / UNCOLLECTED TRANSLATIONS AND POEMS, EARLY AND LATE

DIADEMS AND FAGOTS*

Two Sonnets and Two Fragments by Olavo Bilac,
Translated from the Portuguese by John Meem

DOWN RIVER

The river trembles, rolling, wave on wave . . .
Almost night. Following the slow march
Of the water, which inundates the marshes about it,
We proceed. The wind bends the bamboo trees.

Alive just now, clothed in red, bloody,
The twilight is fainting. The night wipes out
The last light from the firmament . . .
The river rolls, trembling, wave on wave.

ONE EVENING IN AUTUMN

Autumn. In front of the sea. I open wide the windows
Facing the silent garden, and view the waters, absorbed.
Autumn . . . Curling up, the yellow leaves tumble,
They fall. Widowhood, old age, discomfort.

Why, lovely ship, in the light of the stars
Did you visit this sea, empty and dead,
If, at the wind, you lifted your sails,
If, at the light, you left the port?

The water sang. Your sides, kissed by foam,
Broken up in laughter and white flakes.
—But, you came with night and you left with the sun!

And I gaze at the empty heaven; I see the ocean
And the place you were last in
Glowing in the light of dawn.

**Diadems and Fagots* was privately printed in Santa Fé, New Mexico, probably in 1920. It contains the first printed, although not published work of Yvor Winters. Mr Meem has kindly given permission to reprint his translations of the Brazilian poet Olavo Bilac.

WAVES

Between the burning calms, tremulously,
Night on the high seas animates the waves.
From the depths the wet Golcondas rise,
Like pearls: the cold nereids:

Interlock, they run pursued,
Return, crossing themselves; and in lascivious swells
Dress their forms, white and rounded,
With purple algae and sea ferns.

Thighs of vague onyx, polished bellies
Of alabaster, hips of silver foam,
Breasts of uncertain opal, gleam in the night

And green mouths, filled with sighs,
Phosphor-fired and perfumed with amber,
Sob vain kisses which the wind disperses.

THE VALLEY

I am like a valley on a cold evening,
When the souls of the bells, one by one,
In the sobbing good-byes of an 'Ave-Maria'
Expire slowly along the heath.

The Last Sonnets of Pierre de Ronsard

I.

Ill-natured winter nights, Serpents of Alecto,
Fury of the furies, engendered of the earth,
Sisters of Enceladus and of Cocytus' birth,
Do not come near my bed, or quickly turn if so.

What can the sun be doing in the lap of Amphitrite?
Rise up! I pine away, broken by my woes,
But yet I cannot sleep; this evil my life knows,
The greatest evil, brings it still affliction and despite.

In six hours at the least I die with open eyes,
Tossing on my bed and twisting left and right
On one flank, on the other! I storm—none hears my cries.

Unquiet, and unable to hold me in one place,
I call the day in vain, and beg of Death his might;
But Death hears me not, or will not show his face.

II.

Ah, long Winter nights, hang-women, give me now
Patience for this life, and let me go to sleep!
Your very name makes all my body creep
With cold, and then to sweat, so cruelly you go.

Sleep, however slight, makes no wind with his wing
To brush across my open eyes, nor do I own
Strength to close eyelid on eyelid or do aught but groan
In eternal pain, like Ixion suffering.

Old shadow of the earth, but soon the shadow of Hell,
You have raised my eyelids with an iron chain,
Destroying me in my bed with a thousand points of pain.

Oh, bring me death to drive away my sorrows, then;
Ha, Death! the common gate, the comforter of men,
I pray thee with joined hands to come and make me well.

III.

Oh, why sleep, my soul, benumbed, with hidden face?
The trumpet has rung out, pack up your goods and go
Down the deserted road the Christ was first to know
When wet with his own blood he redeemed our race.

It is a hard road and has but little space,
Is followed by few men, the road the bramble fills,
Where rise the poignant heads of the thistle of the hills;
But anyway take courage and do not quit the place.

Do not put your hand against the handle of the plow
That you may start your plow in the middle of the lands,
Looking back forever, time on time, behind your view.

One had better not commence, nor in any wise lift hands,
'Twere better not to plow, so therefore drop your plow;
He who leaves his labor is unworthy of his due.

IV.

One has to leave his orchards and his gardens and his doors,
His platters and his walls that the artisan has done,
And sing of his own funeral in the measures of the swan
Who sings of his own death upon Meander's shores.

'Tis done! I have divided the course of destiny,
I've lived, I've spread my name about sufficiently.
My pen flies up to heaven where it will be a sign
Far from the world's pleasures that take even the fine.

Happy is he who never was; more happy who returns
To nothing, which he was; more happy who sojourns
A man made a new angel beneath the Christ's own eyes;

Letting rot below his booty of the clay,
With which the Fates and Fortune and Destiny may play,
He become all spirit, clean of earthly ties.

OTHER TRANSLATIONS

En un tiempo cogi flores
del muy noble paraiso . . . Alfonso XI (1314?-1350)

OLD BALLAD

from the fourteenth century Spanish

O cold fountain, O cold fountain,   fountain cold with love,
Where the small birds go for joy,   save the turtle-dove.
Though she is widowed and in pain   yet the nightingale
Went with treason to her bough   and began his tale:
'I would be your servant, lady,   should it please you so.'
'Evil are thy words, deceiver,   bitter evil—go!
'I will rest on no bright meadow   nor on flowery bough,
'For if I found the water clear   I find it turbid now.
'I will never take a husband   for I want no son—
'I will have no pleasure of them   nor of anyone.
'End thine evil talk, deceiver,   leave me, traitor, go!
'For I will not be your lover   nor your lady, no!'

—Anonymous

SONNET

from the sixteenth century Spanish

October dragged the dead vines down the path;
And, sullen with the great rains, Iber rose—
Now suffering neither bank nor bridge he goes
And covers all the countryside with wrath.
Moncayo, now as always, stands as one
Crowned with a snowy brow; we scarcely see
The sun rise in the east when suddenly
The thick earth hides it, and we have no sun.

The sea and woods now feel the heavy rage
Of the north wind that locks in with his roar
Dwellers in ports and cabins on the coast.
And Fabius, stretched out before the door
Of Thaïs, weeps for time that he has lost,
With shameful tears that lengthen into age.

—Lupercio Leonardo de Argensola

RONDEAU OF ANTIQUE LOVE

from the sixteenth century French

Long, long ago love led the world away
Without much art or talent—it was gay.
So that a flower given was as fair
As all the round world, for true love was there,
And all the world was in a small bouquet,
Long, long ago.

And if, perchance, the lover had his way,
Ah, do you know how long their love would stay?
Ten years, or thirty years, without a care,
Long, long ago.

Now love is lost, for all that you may say—
Nought but false tears and change have we today.
Nay, would you have me love, first tell me where
True love has gone. I'll be no lover ere
They love again, as then they loved, for aye—
Long, long ago.

Clément Marot

SONG

from the sixteenth century French

He who would be glad
Need only look upon
My lady, who hath had
My Lord Christ's benison.
Hers is so fine a grace
That he who looks at her
May endless grief efface—
Yea, more, if more there were.

No maiden lovelier
Could any wonder make.
The memory of her
Doth start my heart awake.

Her beauty, exquisite,
Hath made me feel of death;
But life is requisite
Where beauty wandereth.

—Clément Marot

THE NEMEAN LION

from the nineteenth century French

After the Conqueror goes into the wood
Following those great footsteps on the ground,
A single roar comes out—the only sound
From that embrace. The sun goes down for good.

Across the brambles and the tangled vines
The startled shepherd into Tiryns flees,
Then turns, to see against the nearest trees,
The great beast poised among the columbines.

He screams. Nemea's terror he has seen
Open his jaws against the bloody sky,
And the sparse mane, and fangs that rise too keen.

For in night's growing shadow there he sees
The frightful hide float over Hercules,
The mingled beast and hero, passing by.

—José María de Heredia

FORGETFULNESS

from the nineteenth century French

The temple is in ruins on the height.
And death has mingled, in the savage grass,
The marble goddesses and gods of brass,
And lonely turf has covered them from sight.

Sometimes a single herdsman comes that way
And with his shell that breathes an old refrain

Fills timeless sea and sky with sound again,
His body black against the azure day.

Earth, the maternal, kind to the old god,
Each spring has made a new acanthus grow
About the crumbling capitals; but no—

Man, still indifferent to the ancient sod,
Hears, without trembling, from the night's slow deep,
The Sea, that mourns the sirens, sink and weep.

—José María de Heredia

POEM IN AUTUMN

from the nineteenth century French

Soon we shall plunge into the shadowy cold.
Farewell, clear light of summers all too short!
I hear below the sombre echoes told
Of sounding wood upon the stony court.

All winter will reënter me: its fell
Anger and trembling, hatred, horror, slow
Labor, and like the sun in polar hell
My heart a reddened block of frozen snow.

Shuddering I hear each fagot fall: the blow
Is duller than a building gibbet's sound.
My soul is like a tower that sinks below
The heavy ram's invariable pound.

I know, rocked by the beating monotone,
That somewhere a great coffin is nailed down . . .
For whom? Today is autumn, summer done!
The sound, of a vast going, moves the town.

—Charles Baudelaire

THE LOST SECRET

from the nineteenth century French

Who will console me? 'I,' said Study. 'See
'Mine endless secrets that shall make thee glad.'
Thenceforth books filled the solitude for me–
I found the world in tears, and still am sad.

Who will console me? 'I,' Adornment said,
'Here are the ribbons and the pearls and gold.'
I slipped the harmless garment o'er my head–
It was my shroud, and I wept as of old.

Who will console me? Travel answered, 'Let
'Me bear thee far away from all thy fears.'
But on old leafy ways my heart was set,
And the new shadows darkened but my tears.

Who will console me? Nothing, now; no soul–
Their voices, nor thy voice; but now descend
Into thy heart, which God has left thee whole.
Or, if he has not, let the matter end.

–Marceline Desbordes-Valmore

THE TOAD

from the nineteenth century French

Singing in a windless night . . .
–The moon inlays with thin and bright
Metal the dark outlined green.
A song; like an echo, quick,
Buried there below the thick
Wood.–Now silence. Come. He's there
In the shadow, there, alone . . .
A toad!
–Come, why this fear
Near your faithful soldier?–Sing!
Shaven poet without wing,
Nightingale of mud . . .

But hear!
—Horror!—He sings.—Horror!!—Why?
Don't you see his eye of fire?
No. Cold, he goes beneath his stone.

Goodnight. The toad you heard was I.

—Tristan Corbière

THRENODY FOR STEPHANE MALLARME

from the nineteenth century French

If one said to you: Master!
Day again!
Here is the dawn once more, the same and pale;
Master, I have left the window clear,
The dawn comes in across the eastern sill,
A day is here!
Then I should think to hear you say: I dream.

If one said to you: Master, we are here,
Alive and hale,
As we were here last evening at your door,
We have come in laughing, and once more
Await the strong embrace and the old look,
Then they would answer us: the Master's dead.

The flowers of my terrace,
Flowers as if between the leaves of a book,
Ah, why the flowers?
Here is some part of us, with this low song of ours
That turns and falls
As these leaves fall and turn—
Here are the shame and anger that it is to live
And say these words—against your tomb.

—Francis Vielé-Griffin

UNCOLLECTED POEMS

LAMENT, BESIDE AN ACÉQUIA, FOR THE WIFE OF AWA-TSIREH*

Two caballeros,
Smooth in the valley,
Laughed—their horses bucked.
The summer foaming.

San Ildefonso
In colors
Faint as dust—
Flower-dripping dancers—
One cannot think
So far away.

And thinking,
Women die,
O Awa-tsireh!

The faded roads
May never move.

Poetry: A Magazine of Verse, September, 1922

*'The Indian in English', a review first published in 1928 and reprinted in *The Uncollected Essays and Reviews of Yvor Winters*, ed. Francis Murphy, contains this reference to Awa-tsireh: 'In an early painting by Awa-Tsireh which hangs on my wall—a row of dancers, twenty-five or thirty, grim-faced and working together—is the accumulated thunder of generations of feet stamping an immediate and magnificent earth.' (p. 42). There are many references to Awa-tsireh of the *pueblo* of San Ildefonso in *American Indian Painting of the Southwest and Plains Areas* by Dorothy Dunn (University of New Mexico Press, 1968). An *acéquia* is an irrigation ditch.

SONNET

The fact that offers neither cause nor gain
Nor a reflection of the mind is God—
Table or chair or spinning shrill tripod,
Prie-Dieu to jazz, will suck you like a drain,
Suck you to shrieking. Real, the writhing grain
Means nothing, makes you nothing, and the room
Laid bare is God, the thinning saline Doom,
Intrinsic cringing of the shadowy brain.

Spin on the tripod, let the music bang!
O metric oracle that found no clause
To regulate the meanings that you sang
When Heaven Doubted Its Eternal Laws!
O you were joyous when the doorbell rang
And God's pure presence froze your bony jaws.

from *The Proof*

THE PROOF

Wayne Ried: died December 1928, Moscow, Idaho

I was not there to see you laid away—
The sudden frame with sudden motion strung
To silence, not to peace, to which there clung
Your mother's image in intenser clay.
Alone, I face my beasts: goat-eyes above
The moment stand, unaltered integer,
The moral being. And I think of her
Whose mind's precision was a way of love.

Before the pure Creative Act—mote-weight
Of brightness added to magnetic bone!—
That, shifting, will quit being and then be,
The mind, incipient, must hesitate;
So you struck hard into the earth, alone,
To prove incalculable Constancy.

from *The Proof*

SHADOWS

In close-locked ranks the day
Of shadows turns; the trees,
Bound to the moment's play,
Are one with these.

Nor yet may man go free;
Though he moves where he will,
The angle with each tree
Falls true and still.

But by the lamp at night
The shadow stands or goes,
It points to left or right,
The blindness grows.

For all is loose to change
And knows nor root nor law;
Cut free from Time they range,
Each thing a flaw.

These are the living dead,
And no one knows his way.
What black fire packs each head
No tongue can say.

from *The Proof*

THE STILL SMALL VOICE

What anger hides
In changing flesh and mind,
The changing heart must find,
The heart decides.

But nought betides.
The heart has found its place
Before her quiet face
And there abides.

O still small word!
The faint report of age
Has one day found the brain!

And he who heard
Turns down the living page
At grief again.

from *The Proof*

SNAPSHOTS

Though moments flee
These few shall stay.
This yesterday
Shall mutiny.

And I shall see
From far away
This flash of play
Grown strange to me.

For we retire,
Yea, sigh by sigh,
Through what is done.

Hard slow desire!
The moments die
Ere peace is won.

from *The Proof*

COMMUNION

The changing mind, like sun that stirs on stone,
Deep in some wooded shade,
Is the incarnate word, grown more alone,
Made and unmade.

Bridging the pure divide, in search of ways
To reach through night and sleep
And bind our fear into the strength of days
So rooted deep.

Up through the climbing miracle of night
Where the heart, still, O still!
Faints far away through all strange calm delight,
Toward deathless will—

There have I been, thence come, and momently
I lay my life aside
That I may lift it up again and be
Thus fortified.

from *The Proof*

THE DEDICATION

To J. L. W.

Confusion, cold and still,
Impeding act and thought,
And the inchoate will;
With these at last I wrought.

Concentered with your mind,
My vision then grew just:
When I no point can find,
I wait, because I must.

Hard study eats to age.
These words are few to show:
I leave them on the page,
Though you alone will know.

from *Before Disaster*

THE ANCESTORS

The wrinkled cypress wall that stands
  Firm till the edges sleep
Thickens its hold on autumn lands
  Grown heavy, deep on deep.

And he who pauses by the gate
  Feels garden beds grow hard
With certainty that gathers late,
  Wisdom that hopes retard.

The dead leave courage for the mind
  To view earth's massy form
In its identity of kind,
  Clean of the changing worm.

from *Before Disaster*

THE WERWOLF

Wolf-bitch who suckled me, the moon
Plays acid havoc in the mist,
And in my veins thy turbid boon
Surges against thee, chaotist.

While he who gave me human eyes
To view the horror of my breast
Lies shrunk to ash, dost thou devise
New ways to desecrate his rest.

Thy face will come from past thy grave
To people my last days with fears.
Thou art confusion. May I save
Some moments from thee, down the years!

Not till his death didst thou resume
The hairy shadow of thy hate,
To flood my veins with sin, a spume
No living tears may dissipate.

from *Before Disaster*

A PETITION

Love is obscure and old.
Unkindness from a past
That you nor I have told
May shade the mind at last.
  When out of nought it shows,
  The sense no lover knows.

Forgive me. From the night
The bitterness of crime,
Irrelevance and flight
Possessed me for a time.
  Loathing my flesh and heart,
  I now lie down apart.

It was not I that spoke;
The wild fiend moved my tongue.
I struggled and awoke
With shame and sorrow wrung.
  Believe me. For my trust
  Will change not in my dust.

from *Before Disaster*

TO HERBERT DEAN MERITT*

Professor of English Philology at Stanford University

on his retirement

Deep in the Cretan cave,
Each golden artifact
Or work in stone or clay
In palace hall or grave
Somehow appeared to stay—
For all the scholar lacked.

But round the buried word
Is only rich decay;
The meanings fall away.
What was it that man heard?
With cool persistent tact
You form what men would say.

*This poem first appeared in *Philological Essays in Honour of Herbert Dean Meritt*, edited by James L. Rosier, published by Mouton.

IV / THE BRINK OF DARKNESS

'The Brink of Darkness' first appeared in *The Hound and Horn* magazine, copyright 1932 by The Hound and Horn, Inc. A different and improved version of the story appeared in *Anchor in the Sea: An Anthology of Psychological Fiction*, edited by Alan Swallow. This version was copyright 1947 by Alan Swallow. The first separate edition of the story, reproduced from *Anchor in the Sea*, appeared in The Swallow Pamphlets Number 15. This is the version given here.

Winters requested that the following statement be offered as prefatory comment: 'Winters says that this story is a study of the hypothetical possibility of a hostile supernatural world, and of the effect on the perceptions of a consideration of this possibility.'

THE BRINK OF DARKNESS

LATE IN October the first snow had come, large heavy flakes with shaggy edges, far apart, moving down in vast circles from a soft sky. The trees in the orchard outside the window of the dining-room were hard and cold, and shone like smooth rock against the earth and the colorless air. And the big rough flakes moved cautiously among them, here and there, as if exploring the terrain. There was a slight flurry, and the flakes gathered faster; then followed flurry upon flurry, a few moments apart, a steady slow pulsation, and with each the air was whiter and darker; till at last, the flurries coming imperceptibly closer and closer together, the air was an unbroken sheet of snow through which one could hardly move, the flakes were small and quick, and darkness, amid the confusion, had superseded twilight.

During the winter months the snow had lain deep over the rounded hills, and I had gone out on skis with my two Airedales. The clouds were of a soft even gray, and they seemed to have no lower edges, so that the sky had no identity—there was merely the soft air. The snow merged into the air from below with no visible dividing line. Often I should not have known whether I was going uphill or down, had it not been for the pull of gravity and the visible inclination of the skis. Often I came to the top of a rise and started down with no warning save the change in speed, or arrived at the bottom of a hill with no warning save the sudden slowing. I could travel for miles and see only one or two houses. Sometimes a mouse appeared, floundering as if in heavy air, and the dogs would lunge clumsily after it, snap it up, and drop it dead, leaving a small spot of blood suspended in grayness; but the few rabbits were better equipped and evaded them.

Once I passed a small pen made of chicken-wire, behind a barn, a pen in which there were fifteen or eighteen yearling coyotes. The farmers often captured the cubs during the spring plowing, and kept them into the next winter in order to slaughter them for the fur. These were about ready for killing. They swung in a group to the fence as I passed, lifting the foreparts of their bodies swiftly and gently, to drop them precisely facing, their shoulders flat, the front legs straight and close together, the wide sharp ears erect, the narrow little noses examining the air detail by detail. It was strange that they never broke through so slight a fence, yet there they were; young dogs would have torn through it with scarcely a pause, scarcely the sense of an obstacle. But these creatures were innocent and delicate, spirits impeded by a spell, puffs of smoke precise at the tips. As I passed, they turned their heads, watching me, then moved away and apart, to lie down in the snow or crawl under their small shelter. They had been the only sign of life amid four hours of snow, and they had made no sound. They had focused upon me for a moment their changing, shadowy curiosity, and then had been dissipated as if by the quiet of the hills.

I remembered the preceding fall. The three of us, myself and the Stones, had been puzzled by the luminosity of the stubble at night. On the slope south of the house, even on moonless nights, it had a curious glow, a kind of phosphorescence, that appeared to light the air for a few inches above the ground and then to stop suddenly. When the moon was full, the glow for several feet above the fields was so dense that the eye could scarcely penetrate to the ground. At a definite level above the field the glow stopped suddenly, and one could look for miles through watery moonlight over hills that seemed smothered in soft fire. The dogs, running through the fire, below the height of visibility, were dark vortices, blurred and shapeless, stirring rapidly in the motionless flame. Above the roof of the house, in the cold nights of late autumn, Orion, the Pleiades, and all the bright powder of the northern heaven, moved steadily from east to west; and the Great Dipper, low to the north, with few stars near it, its large stars plain and heavy, moved with an equal and compensatory pace from west to east and slipped in behind one of the hills.

In spite of the bright autumn and the shadowy winter, the village had been an unbearable blaze of heat in June. The winter wheat, which had germinated and grown eight or ten inches high under the snow, had shot up prodigiously in the spring warmth. The round hills were green, for even the spring crop was well along. The tall elms were in leaf; the apricot orchard about the house was heavy and dark; each tree was a black void growing shadowy and visible at the edges. The summer beat on the ground with no motion. The two white goats across the road lay panting in the shade, trembling watery blotches, barely discernible.

Once the Stones went up into the mountains for the afternoon, taking me with them. The mountains were only ten miles back of the village, and on the way we stopped at a farm owned by Mr Stone and leased to a family of Seventh Day Adventists. The Stones wanted to get the girl of the family to come and help with the housework. She came to the gate with a shovel and a bucket as we drove up, a tall coarse-boned person, somewhere between twenty-five and thirty-five, with sharply drooping and very long shoulders and a small face, snub-nosed and almost featureless, her mouth open. She looked like one who had been intensely preoccupied, and who had discovered us suddenly. She was sweaty and had dust on her clothes and was visibly panting. She promised to come.

During January and the first week in February, the weather was extremely cold. The kitchen range was red hot, and so was the stove in the dining-room, but the corners of the rooms were never warm enough, and in the halls you could always see your breath. I kept my stove on the second floor as hot as I dared, and I usually sat up till one and two in the morning to keep the fire from dying down, for no bed-clothes were adequate. One night the mercury fell to sixty below zero. During this cold spell Mrs Stone took to her bed, become suddenly very weak. She had always been frail; it appeared now that out of humility and consideration for others she had been concealing her weakness till she had arrived at the point where concealment was impossible. Her strength ebbed very rapidly, and as the cold began to grow less savage, she suddenly died.

The undertakers were not allowed to remove her body from the house, for she had not wished it. They came and went. The nurse, a tall, gray-haired woman, asked me to bed the dogs in the barn for a few nights, for the body was to be placed in the hall at the foot of the stairs. The casket was wheeled in, when the undertakers had gone, a soft gray affair, with some sort of lacy material supported above it and dropping away on either side in the form of a tent. From within came the heavy odor of hot-house flowers; as the casket moved, the slight stiff shifting of the body was just visible through the curtain.

Asa Stone, who lived on a neighboring farm, took his father away for the night. The old man, in spite of his bulk, seemed shrunken; his face, pale and lifeless, fell away in heavy lines, and he seldom looked up. Asa led him by the arm to keep him from stumbling.

A neighbour woman came in to sit up with the nurse and myself. The three of us went into the hall and drew back the curtain from the casket. She was dressed in white, her head surrounded by lilies of the valley, her hair, in spite of her sixty years, pure black against the flowers. As we moved the casket a little, there was again the slight stiff shifting of the body. The face was very firm. The jaw was strong, almost too strong for a woman, had it not seemed a strength employed to achieve gentleness. The mouth, wide in proportion to the jaw, suggested her slight smile, but it was not smiling. It was finished. It seemed to have come to an ultimate balance, to have found itself. We dropped the curtain and returned to the dining-room.

Toward morning I went upstairs to lie down for a few hours, for I had to teach during the day. I came down about seven, passed the coffin in the first gray of the dawn, moved through the motionless cold, which seemed to be gathering heavier about it and which was somehow identified with the thin sweet odor, perhaps the odor of death, perhaps of the flowers, of which the casket itself, with its frosty tent, might have been the visible core.

At noon I returned. As I opened the door into the darkened hall, the casket awaited me, the sweet odor deepening on the still air. I was a trifle sickened; it affected me like the smell of ether. I had lunch and returned to my teaching. The casket awaited me in the darkness at five o'clock. In the dining-room the two women were talking and sometimes laughing as they got supper ready. I went up to my room and lay down but could not sleep. I was beginning to shudder a little as I passed the body, yet it was not from fear of the dead. The ghost, if she stood there waiting beside the body, fixing in memory the house in which she had lived for so many years and which she must now leave forever, was too patient, too gentle, to be feared. The thought of her inexpressible solitude filled me with pity.

On the morning after the third night the family began to gather for the funeral. Alvin, the younger son, and his wife, were the first to come, their features obscured with sorrow. Asa and Clara came with Mr Stone between them; the children would be brought over later. Asa's features were those of his mother, but somehow smaller and harder, and with none of her serenity. He was a man who was seldom still for long, who seemed to know little of peace, whether of body or of spirit.

Asa and Clara moved the casket into the parlor and took away the veil. Soon the florist arrived, and I helped him bank the flowers.

In the kitchen there were coffee and a light breakfast for those who needed them. I went out for a cup of coffee. As I entered the kitchen, the Adventist girl from the country came in, her great awkward shoulders drooping and swinging as she moved, her eyes red. Her brother came behind her. He had been deformed from birth. He was over six feet tall, a man of great power and agility, but without forearms; where his elbows should have been, there were thick, red, wrinkled wrists, and on each wrist there were two long red fingers without nails. His nose was long and coarse, and his voice was nasal. To make up for the shortness of his arms, he had developed violent but agile motions of the upper body; doing even the simplest things, he seemed the victim of some unhappy and uncontrollable agitation. He was a teamster by trade, when he had time from his farm, and he often worked for Asa. His abnormality had made him an exile from human society, and as a result he had acquired an unusual sympathy for horses and mules, with whom he could accomplish extraordinary things, and that part of his nature which was not satisfied by this companionship had turned to religion. When driving a team, he sang in a loud nasal drone, almost devoid of variation, hymns which he intended merely to quiet his own spirit, but which, on a still day, could be heard among the hills for a mile or more. He sat at the kitchen table now, as I drank my coffee, his large bony trunk darting suddenly this way and that, his wrinkled fingers squirming about a piece of bread or a knife, his sharp mouth dropping pious ejaculations between swallows. 'Eli can sure talk religion,' Asa had once said of him with admiration.

At the church I sat with the family, in a private room to the side of the pulpit. After the sermon I looked once more into the casket. The black hair seemed not to have stirred. The face was not heavily wrinkled, but there were a few small wrinkles about the mouth and eyes. The skin was preternaturally and evenly white, and in the wrinkles there seemed a trace as of an underlying darkness, even and impenetrable. At the grave, a mile and a half outside of town, the ceremonies were brief, for a vile sleet had set in. The coffin was lowered; the last prayer was read; and the grave was filled with stones and mud. As we drove away, I looked back to see a huge mound of hot-house flowers, dark heavy green, and clear hard white and yellow, lying as if murdered in the colorless air, beneath driving sleet.

That afternoon Alvin and Asa began moving the furniture from the lower part of the house. Two days later they had finished. I was to keep my rooms in the upper part till the house should be sold, since there were only a few months left till the summer vacation. The old man would stay with Alvin. That was late in February. A few days later another heavy freeze set in.

I made no attempt to keep the lower part of the house warm, although I had to use it occasionally. It was absolutely bare. Even the curtains and window-blinds were gone, and when I went down to the kitchen at night for a glass of water, or crossed the parlor and kitchen to reach the basement for coal, I moved through a naked glare of electric light, with wide bare windows on two sides of me, my feet echoing, my hands stiff with the cold. I came to see myself moving in this room, as if from the outside, and I sometimes wondered who I was. When I came home at dusk from teaching and entered the lower hall, I thought I could still feel the earthy cloud at its center. Sometimes my flesh went chill. I came gradually to carry more and more coal upstairs every morning, and soon I was getting enough to last me through the night. Upstairs were the dogs and the stove; below was the echoing desolation.

During the three nights that Mrs Stone had lain below me in the hall, my sensitivity to death, to the obscure and the irrelevant, had been augmented. I felt that I saw farther and farther into the events about me, that I perceived a new region of significance, even of sensation, extending a short distance behind that of which I had always been aware, suggesting the existence of far more than was even now perceptible. This might have unnerved me had it not been for the firmness of the woman in the coffin. In her were united the familiar and the inchoate. The certainty of her expression gave me pause. She was like a friend bidding me be quiet with raised hand, a friend whose bidding I could trust to be authoritative. But with her departure there remained only the demonic silence which she had introduced, and to which for three nights she had given coherence and a meaning.

The dogs, large and unkempt, a mother and her son, were old enough to enjoy spending most of their time on my bed in the cold weather. When I came up the stairs, they would be waiting, their heads on their paws, their faces expressing an identical gentle question. I had kept their bed in another room at first, but the cold had forced me to close the room, and I was glad enough to have the two sleep with me. The field mice from round about were invading the empty building in greater and greater numbers. They were too quick for the dogs at close quarters, especially on the second floor, where there was still a good deal of furniture. The mice lost all fear, and the dogs no longer disturbed them, but would lie still for half an hour, regarding the scratching, shadowy little creatures with indifferent curiosity or remote amusement. During the first week in March, while the cold spell still endured, the dogs did not come one morning when I called them as I was about to leave the house. Nor did they come the next day nor the next. I knew well enough what had happened, and I would not have been greatly troubled had it not been for the weather and a few porcupines in a small wood lot several miles away. Every afternoon I walked over the hills, trying to get a sight of them on the snow. A light snow had fallen after their going, and their tracks had been covered. I did not know how long it might take them to find their way in from among the hills. Here and there a farmer had seen them. They had been living for several days on the offal of a slaughtered calf and had been sleeping in haystacks. Several farmers had tried to catch them for me, but the dogs were powerful, and, when in trouble, as suspicious and nearly as dangerous as wolves. They seemed to be moving in a wide circle, which I gradually mapped, but on which I never intercepted them. If I didn't meet them, at least it was only a question of time till they would pick up my trail and follow me in. The hills were a cold thin blue, darker where the wind had riffled the snow and the earth showed through, their edges definite against the sky with a cold hair-line precision. There were no clouds, and as I returned home at dusk, a few small white stars appearing, the sky stood above me unvaulted, a steely gray, without distance or dimension.

While the dogs were gone, I spent as much of my nights as I could in reading, and when I could no longer read, I took to watching the mice. At first they had seemed to me uncanny, but gradually I came to be fond of them. I put out food for them, and sometimes a dish of milk. With their food they were likely to be boisterous, snatching it and running off, or throwing it about in play if they were not hungry; with their drink they were delicate and gentle, advancing to the rim of the saucer like far-away gazelles, the natives of this dissolving wilderness, their feet as sensitive as ants, their round eyes rolling quickly this way and that.

One night after I had been watching the mice without moving for nearly an hour, I got up suddenly and went downstairs for a glass of water. The sound of my feet rang out with tremendous volume as I descended the stair; as I crossed the glare of the front room, the echo seemed to resound from the room above, as if I were walking up there. I stood still to quiet the noise. I was alone and erect, a few feet from the broad window, bright emptiness behind me. The light from the window fell on the snow outside. It had been warm enough at noon for a slight glaze to form. The shape of the light on the glaze was sharp-edged and clear. Only, at the upper left-hand corner of the window there was darkness, a tangle of withered vines outside. I stared at the smooth surface of the snow thus suddenly revealed to me, like a new meaning not divisible into any terms I knew. Again I had the illusion of seeing myself in the empty room, in the same light, frozen to my last footprints, cold and unmeaning. A slight motion caught my eye, and I glanced up at the darkened corner of the window to be fixed with horror. There, standing on the air outside the window, translucent, a few lines merely, and scarcely visible, was a face, my face, the eyes fixed upon my own. I moved on quickly to the kitchen; the reflection started and vanished.

The next morning, upon reaching my office, I heard of the catastrophe of the night before. One of my students, the son of one of my colleagues, a boy who was to have graduated this spring but who had been confined to the pest-house with meningitis, had, in the night, while no nurse was present, been seized with delirium, had leapt from his bed and escaped from the door of the hospital in his night-clothes. He had run the four blocks separating the hospital and his home, had broken a window and climbed in. An hour later, at midnight, his parents had returned, to find him sitting before a smoldering fireplace in an icy house, moaning to be taken to his room. He had never regained consciousness; before morning he was dead.

There was another funeral in the Presbyterian church. This time the coffin was kept closed, from respect for the disease. The coffin was banked high behind and on either end with yellow chrysanthemums. The boy's fraternity came in a body, twenty and some boys, seated in two front rows at one side, looking curiously young and helpless before the coffin. The waxen petals of the chrysanthemums glowed in the dusk of the church; they seemed almost to move, curling and uncurling ever so little. There was something innocent and pathetic about the flowers, these earthy blossoms, cut clean from the ground from which they had struggled, foaming dimly, still dimly alive in the gloom, struggling imperceptibly, curling imperceptibly inward, as if they were the sluggish dead incarnate, dying slowly again in pity, returning numbly to the earth.

At the end of four days, toward nightfall, the bitch returned, emaciated and limping, her head and throat, inside and out, completely covered with quills, her mouth forced open with the mass of them, her tongue hanging out, swollen, and white with quills as far back as I could see. I was prepared for this kind of return. I held her and poured vinegar over the entire wounded area, to soften the quills. She screamed, but lay still. Had it been the other dog, I would have sent for help and for morphine; I knew that morphine would only make the bitch stupidly savage without calming her, even in doses so large as to be dangerous. I sat astride her body, letting my entire weight fall on her ribs to hold her down. She tossed this way and that, screaming, her mouth foaming with blood. It was strange how hard the things wedged themselves into the cartilage: sometimes I had to pull several times before I could loosen one, and it would come out followed by a gush of blood. The light on the floor was poor and the work was hard; at the end of two hours I was exhausted almost to numbness.

The bitch was panting and weak; sometimes she moaned feebly; the floor was spattered with blood for three or four feet around; but she was clean of visible quills, and few seemed to have buried themselves. I washed her with disinfectant, poured a drink of warmish water into her mouth, and turned her loose. She staggered feebly to her feet and walked over and lay down on the rug behind the stove. The inner surface of her mouth was devoid of membrane, was a bloody pulp, and her head was a clotting spongy mass. It had happened before, and she would survive it; we both of us knew it; she moved her tail feebly, and then cautiously laid her head on her paws. In the morning some boys led the other dog in staggering; they had found him late the night before in the same condition as the bitch, and had taken him to a veterinary before bringing him home.

For the next week most of my free time was spent in nursing the dogs; my bed cover and my rugs were stained with blood; the corners of the room accumulated deeper and deeper dust; the dust lay under the bed in soft whorls; I was busy and very tired and slowly lost the habit of noticing. Once near the end of March, some friends of the Stones from the next town stopped by to see the old man. I explained his absence, and asked them in for a cup of coffee. They came in dubiously, a tall silent old farmer and his gray small wife, the two of them troubled by the combination of my books, of my general affability, and of the dire squalor in which I lived. The dogs sniffed them curiously, extending their raw and scabious heads, and I sent them back to the bed. The old people finally took their leave with great formality.

During the first week in April, Alvin appeared at the door

to say that the house had been sold and that the new owner wished to take possession as soon as possible. I arranged for the room across the street and began to move at once. A Chinook had begun the day before Alvin's appearance and continued for three days; it was the last thaw of the season. On most of the hills the winter wheat was already high, and the hills lay green as the snow vanished. Far across the valley I could hear the puffing of a tractor, and now and then I could see the tiny iron thing crawling rapidly in straight lines across the hills, appearing and disappearing suddenly and in unlikely ways, leaving black earth behind.

Now my belongings were moved, and I would stay in the new house until early June. My new landlord was a teamster with seven children and a tired wife. I should not be with them long enough to become acquainted. The children swarming about the little house bothered me, but I liked them well enough in a way; they were a part of the season. Just outside my door was an old phonograph, which one of the older girls played incessantly. The grass was already green under my new window; the trees were in bud; the two white goats would kid in a week, and the kids, bloody and tottering at first, would be within a few days leaping here and there in the cold shadows, balancing and spinning on a single foot, front or rear, it mattered little, nipping buds they would not care to eat, trying to make friends with the dogs, to the patient embarrassment of the dogs and the consternation of their mothers.

I thought back over the past months, of the manner in which I had been disturbed, uncentered, and finally obsessed as by an insidious power. I remembered that I had read somewhere of a kind of Eastern demon who gains power over one only in proportion as one recognizes and fears him. I felt that I had been the victim of a deliberate and malevolent invasion, an invasion utilizing and augmenting to appalling and shadowy proportions all of the most elusive accidents of my life, my new penumbra of perception thus rendering to what would otherwise have appeared the contingent the effect of coherent and cumulative meaning. Finally, through some miscalculation on the part of the invader, or through some other accident, I had begun to recover the limits of my old identity. I had begun this recovery at the time of the immersion in the brute blood of the bitch. The invading power I could not identify. I felt it near me still, but slowly receding.

I got up from where I sat and stretched myself out in the sun. I was minutely aware of my movements, my inclinations, my bodily functions. I could not blink my eyes without being conscious of the darkness; I knew I was tired. It was as if there were darkness evenly underlying the brightness of the air, underlying everything, as if I might slip suddenly into it at any instant, and as if I held myself where I was by an act of the will from moment to moment. From far over the hills I heard a low snoring drone, rising and falling, as if it came from a lonely bull in a far pasture. A quick and powerful team, four abreast, and drawing a wheel plow, came over the rise at the distance of a quarter of a mile. The plow came down the slope swiftly and started around the base of the hill to circle slowly upward again, the horses arching and rippling, the driver bending forward and moving rapidly here and there to urge them on. From the sound and from the strange movements of the driver, I recognized Eli. I lay back and closed my eyes. The sun poured steadily into me. In a month I should be leaving for Colorado. I would never return.

INDEX OF FIRST LINES